# The Knower Curriculum
## Teach Meditation to Children with Timeless Tales

A perfectionist finishes the task only for knowing that he's perfect
and no gain. Thus continue studies and finish.
(Swami Shyam, 1981, Personal Telegram)

# The Knower Curriculum

## Teach Meditation to Children with Timeless Tales

### Shelley Astrof

# Contents


Foreword    8

How to Use This Book    10

Prologue    15

**Part 1: Curriculum & Instruction**    21

**Chapter 1—The Play of Philosophy, Darshan, Direct Experience**    23
The Mind    24
The Knower    26
Meditation    31

**Chapter 2—The Play of Breath, Pranayama**    38
Awareness of the Breath    39
Pranayama Exercises    41

**Chapter 3—The Play of Sound, Mantra**    58
Mantras    61

**Chapter 4—The Play of Body, Hatha Yoga**    67
Hatha Yoga Poses    70

**Chapter 5—The Play of Action, Karma Yoga**    92
Activities and Games    94

**Part 2: The Play of Words, Implementation**　　151

The Play of Knowledge, Gyan Yoga　　152

Timeless Tales and Their Lessons　　157

Timeless Tale 1—Cunning Mr Monkey　　159
　The Lesson　　162

Timeless Tale 2—Destiny　　172
　The Lesson　　176

Timeless Tale 3—Donkey Riding　　188
　The Lesson　　191

Timeless Tale 4—Fox and Camel　　202
　The Lesson　　208

Timeless Tale 5—Kalpataru　　221
　The Lesson　　224

Timeless Tale 6—The Bribe　　235
　The Lesson　　238

Timeless Tale 7—The Self Fish　　249
　The Lesson　　252

Timeless Tale 8—Truth Story　　263
　The Lesson　　265

Timeless Tale 9—What Is an Elephant?　　276
　The Lesson　　279

Bibliography　　288

Detailed Contents　　290

Afterword　　296

# Foreword

The Knower Curriculum presents a unique and novel approach to the education of children. It is based on the concept of the Knower, the inner consciousness of the child—and indeed of all human beings—which can be introduced to students through definite pedagogical techniques. When the child becomes familiar with the Knower, he or she will grow up to be a peaceful, productive and well-rounded adult.

Ms. Astrof uses stories to which a child can easily relate, to introduce the idea of the Knower. The stories deal with such topics as awareness, justice, alertness, good and bad habits, truth vs lies, being right and at the same time having the ability to see things from another person's point of view and the power of thought—in short, all of those factors which a child will have to deal with throughout his lifetime. The tales and lessons in the book are buttressed by an emphasis on meditation, which is the tried-and-true method for looking inward and coming to know the Knower. Children have the capacity to meditate from a very young age and the cultivation of this habit at an early stage in life will enable them to become successful adults.

Along with her emphasis on meditation, Ms. Astrof also details some yogic disciplines, both physical and philosophical, which aid the child in his development. Practice of these techniques promotes a sound mind and body.

The book's text is accompanied by a companion book for children entitled Timeless Tales, which includes numerous cleverly drawn illustrations which help the students to visualize the concepts which are being taught.

In summary, I would say that this book provides a positive breakthrough in the way children are educated.

Glen Kezwer, Ph.D.

Author of *Meditation, Oneness and Physics* and *The Essence of the Bhagavad Gita*

# How to Use This Book

The field of Curriculum & Instruction is based on research, development and implementation of educational programs designed to increase students' knowledge and achievement both inside and outside of their school experience.

Even with all the technological advancements that our society has to offer, people have not been able to remove their uneasiness and suffering. This book presents a unique curriculum based on the findings of decades of experimentation, meditation, education and study on the Knower. It is the unfoldment of highest awareness and intelligence, which enables a person to remove this suffering through expanding the capacity of the mind while reducing the limitations of its vision.

*The Knower Curriculum* is designed to provide what you need to teach this program to children. It considers the growth and well-being of the whole child as a developing being. In addition it employs the taxonomy of educational objectives[*], which are organized into three domains or areas of concern. These areas are the cognitive, affective and psychomotor domains of education and are traced back to the classical Grecian emphasis on the integration of mental, spiritual and physical development.

The cognitive domain takes into consideration the skills and abilities involved in developing the mind, mental learning and knowledge. The affective domain focuses on the skills involved in developing the child's social and emotional aspects as well

---

* Benjamin S. Bloom, 1956, *Taxonomy of Educational Objectives: The Classification of Educational Goals*

as their attitudes and sense of self. The psychomotor domain considers the skills involved in developing the physical aspects of the child and the use of sensory cues to guide motor activity. It is important for children to manage their energy to help them develop a healthy body, spirit and mind.

The practice of meditation, the ancient yoga disciplines and the knowledge of these *Timeless Tales* will help develop and enhance the child's cognitive, affective and psychomotor domains to make for a happier, healthier and more balanced child.

Meditation for children is so important! It gives them a head start in developing their mind and body awareness as they learn to focus and channel their energy, so that they may become their very best self.

# Part 1
# Curriculum & Instruction

Part 1 Curriculum & Instruction is comprised of five chapters that provide the philosophical foundation, terminology and technical knowledge of how to teach all aspects of this comprehensive program.

This is the learning base for you as teachers and parents. I encourage you to take the time to acquaint yourself with the knowledge and techniques in this part. The depth of your understanding will be transmitted to your students when you implement the curriculum and delve into the realm of the *Timeless Tales*.

**Chapter 1: The Play of Philosophy, Darshan, Direct Experience**
This chapter introduces the philosophical foundation of this curriculum. The three pertinent topics, the mind, the Knower and meditation, are defined and discussed. Understanding the essence of this philosophy is central to the implementation of this program.

**Chapter 2: The Play of Breath, Pranayama**
This chapter focuses on the awareness of the movement of the breath and introduces selected exercises.

**Chapter 3: The Play of Sound, Mantra**
This chapter presents the power of sound and the value of meaning. Specific mantras are also suggested.

**Chapter 4: The Play of Body, Hatha Yoga**
This chapter describes selected hatha yoga poses to enhance the meditation experience.

**Chapter 5: The Play of Action, Karma Yoga**
This chapter is chock-full of activities and games to enhance the themes highlighted in the stories.

# Part 2
# The Play of Words, Implementation

> Everyone wants some magical solution to their problem and everyone refuses to believe in magic.
> (Lewis Carroll, 1865, *Alice in Wonderland*)

**The Play of Knowledge, Gyan Yoga**
This is where the magic happens. Where meditation, knowledge, yoga and activities come together as a whole under one umbrella, *Timeless Tales*. Part 2 consists of nine insightful stories, each is coupled with its own lesson.

**Timeless Tales**
Every timeless tale can stand on its own so you can easily read and reread each one to your class at any time. As well each tale is paired with a lesson that highlights its theme and presents discussion ideas and questions. Each lesson also includes something from every chapter presented in Part 1 Curriculum & Instruction. Familiarity with the philosophy, terminology and methodology enhances the delivery of the lesson.

**The Lesson**

**Theme:**
The specific topic of the story is stated and examined.

**Discussion:**
This section includes dictionary definitions of pertinent words as well as guidelines for discussions.

**Suggested Discussion Questions:**
A list of suggested questions is provided to enhance class discussions.

**Meditation:**
Specific meditation techniques are offered to match the theme of the story.

**The Play of Breath, Pranayama:**
Suggested breath exercises are listed to complement the story theme. Specific instructions on how to perform the breath exercises are found in the chapter "The Play of Breath, Pranayama."

**The Play of Sound, Mantra:**
This section offers mantras—the power of sound and meaning—to enrich the story theme. Specific mantra instructions are found in the chapter "The Play of Sound, Mantra."

**The Play of Body, Hatha Yoga:**
Children can stretch and strengthen their body with theme-related hatha yoga poses. Specific instructions on how to perform the poses can be found in the chapter "The Play of Body, Hatha Yoga."

**The Play of Action, Karma Yoga:**
Included in this section are a variety of games and activities appropriate for school-age children. Suitability of the games and activities will depend on the age and ability of your students. The instructions for these activities comprise the chapter "The Play of Action, Karma Yoga."

These *Timeless Tales* offer an opportunity for children to grow and develop. Through the practice of meditation, guided discussions, yoga disciplines and activities, the whole child is enriched and refined.

Watching children blossom is the real magic. And this is where it happens.

Enjoy!

# Prologue

Any education which allows man to grow and awaken
the nature of the Self, the Inner Reality, will be a profound
educational system.
(Swami Shyam, 1988, International Conference On Education)

Everywhere all over the world, in every age, in every time, at every stage stories have been told and retold. Over time stories have been passed along to express events, share experiences, teach lessons and give instructions.

Firstly, I'd like to thank you for your interest in teaching meditation to children. *The Knower Curriculum* along with these *Timeless Tales* will take you on a voyage of unlocking wisdom. You will journey from the mind to meditation, from thoughts to stillness, from sound to silence and from worry to peace, where you will come to meet your own Self, the Knower.

This curriculum is one that is very close to my heart and has been many, many years in the making. These pages are steeped in the knowledge and fragrance of my love and dedication to this project. With extensive research, I offer my knowledge and years of experience in the fields of education, meditation and yoga disciplines and my years of collecting insightful stories for children and grown-up children.

I first heard these stories from my cherished teacher, Swami Shyam. He was a master of the art of telling tales, a genuine raconteur with a knack for expressing the ineffable. He could spin a yarn that would bring joy and delight to his ready listeners, while expanding their vision, knowledge and awareness. This book is dedicated to his living wisdom, knowledge, love and absolute delight.

He always said that we grow best through joy and delight. When asked, "Don't we grow through suffering?" he would playfully reply, "Through suffering, we grow into more suffering, and through joy, we grow into more joy." With wit, wisdom, humour and charm, he masterfully led our attention towards the one who is watching, listening and knowing; delightfully informing us that the nature of watching and knowing is joy and freedom.

As a parent and educator I pondered over how to achieve a balance between freedom and discipline. Dictionaries* define freedom as "the condition of not being bound, affected or restricted." Swami Shyam described "real freedom" as having discipline contained within it. He said that real freedom is achieved through knowledge and guidance. To illustrate his point he used the example of a river. He said that a river has two banks, knowledge and guidance. It is these two banks that give the water its shape and form. When water is in the form of a river, then it is able to flow freely, easily and directly to its source.

In appreciation of the joy, wisdom and delight that Swami Shyam brought to my life and to the many lives he touched, I thought to include the word "play" in each chapter title. These stories come from that place that is beyond time and space. They are presented to the listening mind, introducing the awareness of the unchanging Knower to all who have ears to hear.

> Be yourself; everyone else is already taken.
> (Unknown source, attributed to Oscar Wilde)

I have always loved stories. One of my fondest childhood memories is sitting in my room with crayons and a colouring book, listening

---

* All dictionary meanings are from: dictionary.com, dictionary.cambridge, en.oxforddictionaries.com, merriam-webster.com, wikipedia.org.

to those 78 rpm records that played the narration of so many stories and fairy tales on our portable record player. I spent so many wonderful hours sitting on that hardwood floor, listening and colouring with my crayons. I remember how much I loved to listen to a particular storyteller who had the most wonderful voice. As I listened to her read the stories, her voice would transport me to a place that seemed to be out of time and space. I remember feeling absorbed in a wonderfully sweet and beautiful space that felt like my true home.

I was quite young and had my own very definite ideas about how the world and things worked, even though I had not completely thought things through. How did that lady with the lovely voice manage to fit inside the record player, and how did she keep up with my story selections?

One of those magical moments listening to a story record was the first time in my life that I had the experience that my mind got blown. I remember it so clearly. My mind became overloaded with opposing, conflicting thoughts and ideas of what I believed reality to be. These opposing beliefs collided with one another and presented an alternate reality to the one I believed to be true.

My older brother was watching television in the living room of our house. When I opened the door of the room I was in and took my first step into the open hallway, I was suddenly thunder-struck. Echoing through the hallway was the unmistakable voice of that lovely lady, coming from the television set. How could that be! How could she be **in** my record player **and in** the television set at the same time? The world I believed in was suddenly in question.

I can remember standing still for the longest time trying to resolve this paradox. This was the first time I experienced my concepts and ideas, which I believed to be true—my world, my beliefs, my ideas, my thoughts, my reality—they were all being challenged.

I'm sure many of you who are reading this can remember a time or moment when your own beliefs, true thoughts and real ideas came into question.

It's interesting to note that people can believe in a reality as truth without actually knowing that they believe it. They just take it for granted. In fact, until or unless a person's beliefs are challenged, they may not even be aware that they hold that belief or idea, as truth.

These *Timeless Tales* may make you think about things and situations in new, different and even challenging ways. Some stories may call into question ideas, thoughts and concepts that you may not have realized you held as truth. Thus, these stories can provide a platform for expanding the confines of your mind's ideas, concepts and thinking.

But best of all these amazing *Timeless Tales* will bring delight and joy to the reader and the listener.

> Meditation is a method or technique of educating the human mind, of giving it greater capacity and greater power of understanding. (Swami Shyam, 1994, *Vision of Oneness*, p 175)

Children gather strength by closing their eyes in meditation. They centre themselves and get in touch with their essential nature, which lies at the core of their being. When knowledge is added to meditation, children have the opportunity to develop new perspectives and explore dimensions of their minds and personalities. These *Timeless Tales*, along with knowledge and activities, help children to develop their own power, clarity and executive ability.

The rhythm of consciousness is the governing power of this curriculum. It goes by the name "Knower." The Knower is realized through the knowledge and practice of yoga. Dictionaries define yoga as union. They also state that yoga is the union of the limited self with the divine Self. However, the aim of yoga is not to unite people with something that is other than who they are. The aim of yoga is to uncover and discover who they already are—they already are their own Self, the Knower.

Yoga is also defined as a group of physical, mental and spiritual disciplines which originated in ancient India. To amplify meditation, *Dhyan Yoga,* and to help unfold the Knower, I have included a number of yoga practices as chapters. "The Play of Breath, Pranayama," balances the body and mind so it remains healthy and balanced, and creates a great ease for meditation. "The Play of Sound, Mantra," strengthens the power of concentration and releases the mind from scattered, consuming energy, thus creating a concentrated space for meditation. "The Play of Body, Hatha Yoga," develops strength in the body and mind, which gives the child more power and focus to sit in meditation.

In these chapters I wanted to honour the ancient tradition of yoga and so for each of the poses and exercises, I have included the original Sanskrit names in addition to the names they are known by in English.

> The colours of the rainbow are only in our eyes. The rainbow
> has no colours, it is only sky.
> (Swami Shyam, Unpublished Discourse)

These *Timeless Tales* along with the practice of meditation will help children learn how to watch and examine their minds. They will discover what suits them and what does not. They will learn to have confidence and flexibility in their decisions. They will learn to have independence in their thinking, certainty in their abilities, discrimination in their judgement and impeccability in their actions. They will have the courage to make proper choices so they can live a happier, healthier and more joyful life. This is the precious gift of *The Knower Curriculum.*

> But, I nearly forgot, you must close your eyes otherwise you
> won't see anything. (Lewis Carroll, 1865, *Alice in Wonderland*)

Enjoy!

# Part 1
## Curriculum & Instruction

1. The Play of Philosophy, Darshan, Direct Experience
   - The Mind
   - The Knower
   - Meditation

2. The Play of Breath, Pranayama

3. The Play of Sound, Mantra

4. The Play of Body, Hatha Yoga

5. The Play of Action, Karma Yoga

# Chapter 1
# The Play of Philosophy, Darshan, Direct Experience

Through meditation one learns that the normal waking state
of consciousness can no longer be, by any means, the standard
of judging the nature of all things.
(Swami Shyam, 1974, *The Sovereign Secret of Meditation*, p 3)

Darshan, direct experience, is the philosophical foundation of *The Knower Curriculum*. The three main philosophical aspects are the mind, the Knower and meditation. They are so intertwined that I decided to create a single chapter that embraces all three. I wanted to define the differences and examine the thread that makes these three aspects one.

Only the human child is the representative of the offspring
that inquires or wants to know more and more.
(Swami Shyam, 2015, *You Are Never Ignorant of Your Self*, p 1)

When the body is born the senses are included. The child's mind, intellect and ego begin to appear as a kind of sprout consciousness. As children grow into body awareness, the senses and mind develop a power of consciousness and the children want to know about all the things that appear in the world before them: what they see, hear, taste, touch and smell. At this stage children ask, "What is this?" and receive answers in terms of the names of the objects in question.

There are also subtler, abstract and unobvious perceptions, which children begin to feel and think about as they develop in their childhood. This power of consciousness has no form, yet it also exists. In order to understand the subtler powers of consciousness—such as the experience of happiness and unhappiness, joy and pain, feeling easy and uneasy—the same method of inquiry may be used, where the child can ask, "What is this?" Children may even begin to wonder why pain and suffering have entered their lives, and how this sense of pain, uneasiness and confusion can be removed. They may also wonder how they can be happy all the time.

*The Knower Curriculum* is a definite process that requires time, patience, deep thinking, study and meditation for its unfoldment. It offers the children time to be with others and time to sit quietly with their own inner Self. It offers them time to just be.

# The Mind

> Whenever peace arises, challenge your mind to remain in that state. (Swami Shyam, Unpublished Writing)

Dictionaries define the word "mind" as the part of a person that makes it possible for him or her to think, feel emotions and understand things.

Teachers should know how to expand the minds of children by developing their thinking. The first step in expanding the mind is to understand what the mind is and how it functions.

The mind is an amazing instrument that receives its input from the five senses (sight, sound, taste, touch and smell) as well as from parents, family, society, events and circumstances. You might say that the mind is like a camera, in that it can record images but it cannot know that which is beyond itself—the camera cannot know the photographer, the one who is taking the photo.

The mind is a mechanism whose nature and function is to perceive. Based on the input the mind receives, it processes, develops, cultivates and influences a person's personality, ideas, concepts and understanding. The result of this perceptual input is what we call thoughts, ideas, concepts and conclusions. Very often we believe these to be the truth, the real truth.

With every sensation it receives, the mind accommodates, assimilates and incorporates the new input. It then alternates between affirming and negating its position. We come to know that the mind is a mechanism that adapts to greet its ever-changing situations, circumstances and inputs.

Mind is meant for learning and learning is defined as a process of acquiring knowledge. And the process of acquiring knowledge is dependent on the input that comes from the senses, environment and company. The mind helps children navigate through their world of thoughts, feelings, happenings, decisions and interactions. Even before children become aware of the mind, they may feel that their minds are nice to them and conclude that they are good, kind and fair. Sometimes they feel that their minds are not nice to them and conclude that they are bad, unkind and unfair. Thinking and concluding is the mind's function; however, when they think that their mind is not nice it makes them feel weak, miserable and worthless, and as a result they suffer. And no one wants to suffer.

> The world only exists in your eyes. You can make it as big or as small as you want. (F. Scott Fitzgerald, 1925, *The Great Gatsby*)

It is interesting to observe that suffering occurs because of a thought, and happiness occurs because of a thought...and thoughts are changing...and the changing thoughts are coming from a changing vehicle, the mind...

Children don't have to be at the mercy of every thought that pops into their heads. **They can choose**. Children have the power to choose. They don't have to feel bullied, certainly not by other people, but most definitely they don't have to feel bullied by their own minds and the thoughts that make them suffer. They can make their minds a friend, and give their minds the kind of charm and appreciation that results in peace and delight. Meditation helps.

You may have heard people say that you should control the mind and thoughts—even though it often feels like the mind and thoughts are controlling you. Trying to control the mind is like trying to catch the wind in your hands. In fact, you should not try to control the mind at all. Rather, you should try to get in touch with that true freedom that is already inside you.

With the help of meditation, you get acquainted with the part of yourself that is unchanging, as you learn to allow the mind to become absorbed in the peace of your own true nature, the Knower. In this way, the Knower-inspired mind will naturally shine with the light and delight of the infinite Knower. As a result you will live the state of real happiness, freedom, peace and bliss.

# The Knower

> When the mind is out of the way, the Self responds to its own name. (Swami Shyam, Unpublished Writing)

The nature of the Knower is intelligence and delight, which exist in every child. This intelligence shines through the mind yet is not bound by the mind. Rather, it is the grasping power through which things are known. The aim of this curriculum is to unfold the intelligence of the child so it will unite the mind with its own source, the Knower.

Through the process of watching in meditation, children develop the capacity to observe their own thoughts and thinking patterns, while remaining the uninvolved observer or Knower of their own thinking. When children become aware, they come to know that the Knower has the power to guide them through every situation.

Children first need to understand that they have minds, but they are not defined by their minds or bound by the confines of their own thinking. The mind is always changing because it is dependent on the input it receives from the outside via the senses. Mind then adapts to greet the ever-changing circumstances, happenings and situations that come before it. That is why our thoughts are constantly changing. But what children think and conclude with their minds is not who they are. It is what they think.

So the question may arise, "If they are not what they think and conclude, then what are they?"

The query can be considered as, "Who is the one who is thinking?" You might answer, "I am thinking."

"Who is this 'I' and what happens to this 'I' when you are asleep?" You might answer, "I don't know."

So, who is this 'I' who does not know?

At this moment, in order to address and answer these queries, I would like to pause to introduce the four states of consciousness.

## The Waking State:

This is the state of consciousness where you live your life. Where you act, think and interact. The waking state is the movement of the mind, where all your senses are operational. In the waking state, **mind rules**.

The mind rules the field of time and space, where everything has a beginning and an ending. In the mind's waking state all your thoughts, ideas and concepts appear and are seen and experienced as your true reality for some time. In due course they dissolve or disappear, making way for new thoughts and ideas to appear. This is the natural law that belongs to time and space, which is the field of the mind and the waking state.

Thus, the mind's waking state is considered to be a changing field of consciousness, where you work and play and grow and change. My teacher calls the waking state the **long dream**.

## The Dream State:

In the dream state of consciousness, the mind also manifests thoughts, ideas and experiences that appear to be real. The dream state is of shorter duration than the waking state, yet when one is engaged in a dream it feels very real during the time that the dream is taking place. The dream state is also time-and-space bound, which means it appears, stays for some time and in due course disappears. Also, in the dream state, **mind rules**.

> We are such stuff as dreams are made on,
> and our little life is rounded with sleep.
> (William Shakespeare, 1611, *The Tempest*, 4.1)

I love this passage from Shakespeare because it really rounds out the perception of what the dream state is. Suppose you had a dream that you were having a great time with lots of friends. Every one of those dream friends would be made of such stuff that the dream was made of. But what is the dream made of?

It is only when you wake up from the dream that you realize that it was a dream, which means that it was not real so far as the waking state is concerned. This brings us to ask, What is real? When you wake up from the dream and deep sleep states, what do you wake up to? Normally you say that you wake up to the mind's waking state, which is what you call real or reality.

The dream state is a kind of metaphor for the waking state, which is a long dream that you can also wake up from. But what do you wake up to? We'll talk about that soon.

The next state I'll present is the state of deep sleep.

## The Deep Sleep State:

In this state of consciousness, the mind is quiet. You might say that it is absorbed in sleep, or the mind is asleep. You are still alive, yet the mind is not functioning as it does in the waking and dream states. The perception of the deep sleep state is that it is out of time and space. While you are asleep you have no idea as to the passage of time. You only know that time has passed when you wake up.

During deep sleep, you remain undisturbed by the aches and pains and happenings of the dream and waking states where mind rules. When you are in deep sleep, if someone calls your name, you don't respond, because you as mind don't hear it. You, as mind, are not there to hear it. But you as you are still alive. You as you are still there. This brings us to the next state, the fourth state of consciousness, the Knower state.

We can wake up to this state!

## The Fourth State:

This is the state of Knower, the state of Self that remains stable, unchanging, eternal and ever-present. It is there before the mind wakes up in the morning and after the mind goes to sleep at night. It is the background state on which the other three states—waking, dream and deep sleep—reside. The Knower state is always present, quietly and subtly remaining unnoticed as the background space. This state is out of time and space. It is eternal, unchanging and forever.

The Knower state is like the background canvas on which the artist paints his or her masterpiece. When viewing a painting, most often you only pay attention to the forms, objects, colours, brush strokes and background spaces of the painting. But a painting cannot exist without the canvas on which it is painted. That background canvas is analogous to the state of the Knower. The artist's canvas is there before the artist begins to apply the colours to the canvas. In this way, the Knower state is there as the canvas of life, before the mind and senses begin to apply their colours in the forms of thoughts, concepts, ideas and perceptions, that paint our individual lives on the Knower canvas.

> Who in the world am I? Ah, that's the great puzzle.
> (Lewis Carroll, 1865, *Alice in Wonderland*)

It is possible to wake up from the mind-ruled states of consciousness that are grounded in the field of time and space and place. The mind-ruled states have borders which we call birth and death, appearance and disappearance, and beginning and ending. The state of Knower has no borders.

The Knower gets blocked in the waking state, and as a result objects, relations, and time and space appear to be real, so they become most important. Meditation unblocks the Knower, which allows the mind to become steeped in the fragrance of the Knower. When you align yourself with the unchanging eternal nature of the Knower, you operate from that place that is out of time and space, and out of the mind field that is constantly changing. In this state, the mind is infused with the steadiness of the peaceful, unchanging nature of its Knower source. And as a result, you function much, much better.

Meditation as a curricular technique is the practical application for the direct experience of the Knower.

# Meditation

> Meditation is being conducted to allow the Knowledge to appear in you. This Knowledge is the awareness which you are missing, and with which you will be able to know who you are. (Swami Shyam, 1975, *Mastermind*, p 29)

Meditation is an ancient practice, a science and philosophy that is called *Dhyan Yoga* in Sanskrit. It refers to the entire process of evolving the intelligence of a human being to the state of Self-realization, the Knower state of consciousness.

Meditation is simple to do and easy to learn, but to master it and receive its full benefits requires regular practice and knowledge of its process. The mind will know the result of meditation in the form of joy, peace and the sense of freedom from doubt and confusion. And the body will become healthier and happier. So, for those interested in their well-being, the practice of meditation is important.

Any time is a good time to meditate. You don't have to be punctual, or sit for an exact number of minutes, at an exact time, but regularity is a must. Regularity is most essential because meditation is a kind of power that builds on itself.

It is through the practice of meditation that the Knower is revealed. Placing the attention on the one who is having the thoughts—rather than becoming involved in the thoughts that are coming and going and constantly changing—builds a great power. And that power is built through regularity.

While meditating you might find that at the back of your closed eyes, thoughts appear. Thinking in meditation can be transformed into knowing, as you come to realize that there is a Knower of the mind and senses. Through the continued practice of meditation, we discover that spaces, sounds and thoughts may appear, change and disappear, but the Knower who knows and watches them, remains constant and unchanging.

When thoughts arise, simply observe them coming and going with gentle watchfulness, knowing that your observation does not cause them to arise in your mind. Thoughts come uninvited; you didn't create them. Thoughts appear and will stay for some time and then go away. You don't have to interfere with the freedom of their departure. Just remain free and watching, like the sky that remains free even though many birds and airplanes fly in it.

Let the thoughts come and go and rise and subside, while you quietly watch as the witness. Remain uninvolved in the company of your own well-being. This is your true Self, the Knower, who you meet in meditation.

I remember the first time I was in an airplane. My mother and I flew from Montreal to New York. I was quite young and everything was so new and exciting and kind of scary at the same time. It was a very stormy day, and even though it was morning, the sky was dark and heavy with clouds. The rain was pounding on the propeller plane as we sat on the runway waiting to take off. I'll never forget the feeling I had when the airplane climbed higher in altitude. I sat mesmerized looking out that oval window as the roads and cars and houses began to look like miniature toys on a dark, wet earth. When the airplane pierced through the cloud-cover, suddenly it was sunny, very, very sunny. All the houses, cars and roads were gone, and below us was just a dark mist. I remember my mother saying that we were now flying above the clouds. "Wow, above the clouds..." I wondered if it was always sunny above the clouds.

Meditation is like being above the clouds where the light of the Knower is forever shining its delight.

Through the practice of meditation you come to know that the one who observes your thoughts is you, the Knower; the one who knows you slept well in deep sleep is the Knower; the one who sees in the dream state is the Knower; and the one who perceives in the waking state is the Knower.

The Knower is the unchanging background canvas, whose nature is freedom and delight. Through meditation, the mind becomes absorbed and coloured in its unchanging light and delight. Then whatever the mind sees, perceives and understands is coloured in the light, delight and freedom of the Knower space. In this way the Knower space becomes the mind's playground.

The knowledge of the Knower is unfolded through meditation.

## How to Meditate

> To find the unobvious, we close the eyes. Then we celebrate
> the Source of Me. (Swami Shyam, Unpublished Writing)

Several techniques can be used in a single meditation. Just be comfortable and easy, and the results will be marvellous. I have included several techniques as chapters in this book.

The chapter called "The Play of Breath, Pranayama" introduces breathing techniques that can be used as breath exercises on their own or during meditation.

The chapter called "The Play of Sound, Mantra" introduces a variety of mantras that children can repeat during meditation to enhance and focus their meditation experience.

The children can meditate while the stories are read aloud. Listening to these timeless tales that are filled with knowledge and wisdom can open their minds to new vistas, fresh ideas and different viewpoints. This will help them expand and explore their own vision and understanding.

To introduce meditation to children, you can ask them to make a comfortable seat anywhere and close their eyes. You can let them know that their eyes will know that there is nothing in front of them. Yet, in their minds the memory of things and persons that were seen and experienced, is still there. All that is known by the mind and senses, is filtered into the mind, processed, understood and made into a formed, mental, believable reality.

Memory is a human mental sense. The mind sees through memory even when the eyes are closed and not seeing outwardly. During the process of sitting in meditation, the mind may carry on thinking for some time. The purpose of meditation is to wait and watch and observe the mind's patterns, activities and thoughts as if they were clouds in the sky of the mind or characters on a television screen who are just figures of light. The one who is watching and knowing the mind is your own Self, the Knower.

It's important to note that meditation is not about trying to get rid of the mind, or trying to make it be active or quiet. If you don't like what comes before your eyes, you don't condemn them for seeing it, and you don't condemn your ears for hearing what you don't want to hear. Similarly, you don't condemn your mind for the thoughts that come before it. The eyes and ears are simply part of the sensory apparatus of the human mechanism. So too is the mind. The mind takes its input from the senses, and also takes cues from parents, teachers, friends, family, television, movies, apps and all that comes in front of it.

Meditation is about sitting quietly and comfortably with closed eyes. In due course, the other senses naturally quiet down. The children can be taught that there are several techniques they can use to make their meditation fabulous.

So have them sit quietly, watch and wait. Whatever thoughts, memories or ideas have come, will also go. They should be with the one who is watching, knowing and never changing. That is the Knower. Be with the Knower.

The purpose of meditation is not attained by the absence of the mind, or by calling that absence peace. Rather, the practice of meditation unfolds the original sense of Existence and Consciousness, which is the source of all individual forms, sentient and insentient, in existence.
(Swami Shyam, 2012, *Highest Wishfulfiller Meditation Explained*, p 9–10)

## Other Approaches to Meditation for Children

There are no foreign lands. It's the traveler only who is foreign.
(Robert Louis Stevenson, 1883, *The Silverado Squatters*)

There is an increasing interest in meditation for children, which is evidenced by the appearance of so many meditation courses available on the internet and through community and yoga centres. Many bookstores now feature numerous books and materials on meditation for children.

There are also many articles and research projects documenting the benefits and value of meditation for school-age children. These programs explore and examine an abundant array of research that delves into the many advantages and rewards of meditation for children. They also mention the effects meditation has on the school environment—from improving the mental, emotional, social, physical and academic performance of the students, to changing the tone of the school atmosphere.

One of the leading proponents of meditation for children is Mindfulness Meditation. They have published extensive research studies which were carried out in a variety of home, school and after-school settings. Other great advocates of meditation programs, apps and resources for children are Transcendental Meditation, the Chopra Center, Headspace, The Hawn Foundation's Mindup, Kids Yoga Stories and Yoga Journal, to name a few.

I love reading about these programs and the many benefits that meditation has had on the lives of young people. It warms my heart. I have so much respect and admiration for all these groups and programs because they do so much to promote meditation for children at home and in schools. The research is extensive and gratefully appreciated.

The uniqueness of this program, *The Knower Curriculum,* is the introduction of the Knower. Knower meditation transforms the mind's waking state of consciousness into the Knower state of consciousness as the child attends the Knower. Through this technique, the mind becomes steeped in the light and delight of its own unchanging Self, the Knower. In Knower meditation the mind, which operates according to its input, becomes saturated with the input of the unchanging state of delight, peace and intelligence—the nature of the Knower. The mind then operates from this vision, transforming its outlook to the delight, peace and wisdom of the absolute unchanging Knower state.

I remember my teacher, Swami Shyam, saying that when he was a young boy, his own teacher told him that he should meditate regularly, every day. His teacher promised him that if he meditated every day, three things would happen for him:

1.  He would always pass his exams.
2.  He would always be healthy.
3.  Everyone would love him.

These promises most definitely came to pass.

No matter what meditation technique you prefer or practice, the most important thing to remember is to meditate. Just meditate! Meditate regularly and you will see, the benefits will come.

It pleases, delights and excites me to see meditation being introduced to children in schools, in after-school programs and at home. It is reassuring to know that the well-being of children is being addressed. I feel so delighted to be able to combine and share with you my favourite things in one book—my love for children, meditation and stories.

When I was an elementary school teacher, I loved our story-time. I loved to watch my class children curl up and listen as the tales unravelled and we were all transported to the place from where the story came.

> You have brains in your head.
> You have feet in your shoes.
> You can steer yourself any direction you choose.
> (Dr. Seuss, 1990, *Oh, The Places You'll Go!*)

Enjoy!

# Chapter 2
# The Play of Breath, Pranayama

> What I want to prescribe for everyone is a practical method of
> how to get connected to the centre of your *pran* or source of
> your energy, which is in abundance.
> (Swami Shyam, 2008, unpublished discourse)

Pranayama, the play of breath, is an ancient yogic practice. The word pranayama comes from two Sanskrit words: *prān*, which means vital life force, energy or the power that moves the breath; and *ayam* which means to channel, exercise or elongate. The practice of pranayama means to channel the power that moves the breath.

*Prān* moves by itself. You know that you breathe in and breathe out, but most often you breathe without being aware of it. The *prān* or energy is hidden in the breath as the power that moves it. You only come to know the *prān* through the breath that is moved. *Prān* is powerful, it is connected to the Knower, and it works to keep the body, mind and senses healthy. Using the breath as its instrument, the *prān* animates the body and the senses.

The practice of pranayama directs and enhances the power of the *prān* through a variety of exercises or techniques. When practiced correctly, these techniques make the mind and body easy and balanced, without worry, tension and agitation. Through awareness of the breath, you learn how to focus the power of the *prān* for your own well-being.

The movement of breath is linked with the movement of the mind. You may have noticed that when a person is upset, angry or scared his or her breathing is rapid and shallow; and when a person is relaxed and calm his or her breathing is deep and steady. Breathing patterns are altered in response to emotional and mental input, which illustrates that thoughts and emotions affect breathing—and breathing affects thoughts and emotions.

It is important to bring awareness of breath to the children's notice, so they can attend and observe the rhythm of their own breathing. Each child is unique and differs from others in his or her own nature, temperament and personality. That is why it is most important that each individual child discover his or her own rhythm, pattern of breathing and level of comfort.

# **Awareness of the Breath**

No one can tell me,
Nobody knows,
Where the wind comes from,
Where the wind goes.
(A.A. Milne, 1927, "Wind on the Hill," *Now We Are Six*)

Bringing the children's attention to the fact of their breath is central to their becoming knowledgeable about their *prān*. You can ask the children to sit comfortably and observe their own breath by paying attention to its movement. The children can watch as they breathe in and out. Through this inflow and outflow of air the body maintains its balance. The children can sit quietly and pay attention to their own individual rhythm of breathing.

You can bring their attention to what happens after they breathe out and before they breathe in. They will notice that there is a pause before the breath changes direction from exhalation to inhalation and from inhalation to exhalation. This pause is called *kumbhak* and it plays an important part in the pattern of breathing. The children can watch as they check the rhythm of their own inclination of breathing in, pausing, breathing out, pausing and so on.

They will come to know that their breath was already there, already moving—inhaling, pausing, exhaling, pausing, inhaling, pausing, exhaling, pausing etc.—before they began to watch their breath. This observation will give the children the experience of the changing nature of the breath.

You can direct their attention to the one who is watching the breath. The one who is watching the breath is the Knower. The unchanging Knower is the background space that is creating the breath, moving it, regulating and looking after the whole system.

The play of breath exercises should always be approached with ease and gentleness. The children should never push themselves or overdo an exercise. It is most important, rather it is essential, that they always, always follow their own breath pattern. If a child has any feelings of discomfort while doing any breath exercise, have him or her **stop** practicing immediately. While performing pranayama exercises, the children should never force their breath.

It is important to build each exercise slowly. The play of breath is not a competition. Rather, it is the feeling of ease, safety and comfort that is most important when introducing and practicing pranayama exercises. Please remind the children to breathe through their nose if they can unless indicated otherwise. This will achieve the best results.

Practicing pranayama on a regular basis brings calmness, balance and stillness to the children's mind and body inspiring them to be aligned with their own true Self, the Knower. It prepares the mind to respond to stress, anxiety and discomfort, by calming the mind's restlessness. It is also a wonderful preparation for meditation.

Pranayama meditation is a marvellous technique. It is the conscious awareness of watching the movement of breath in meditation. It aligns the meditator with the one who is breathing—and the one who is breathing is you, the Knower.

P.S. To enhance meditation on breath, the use of a mala is a great technique to focus and concentrate the mind. (see Mala in The Play of Action, Karma Yoga)

# Pranayama Exercises

I have included some pranayama exercises for teaching and practicing the play of breath with children. The names of the pranayama exercises are presented in English, Sanskrit and transliteration. I am presenting the original Sanskrit names to honour the ancient tradition of yoga, from where they came. It is certainly the choice of the teacher to decide which name she or he is comfortable with. Whichever name you choose, the exercise remains the same.

> What's in a name?
> That which we call a rose
> By any other name
> would smell as sweet.
> (William Shakespeare, 1595, *Romeo and Juliet*, 2·2)

It is important to always begin pranayama with awareness—to have the children quietly watch the natural rhythm of their own breath before beginning any exercise. In this way they come to know where they are starting from and what changes happen to their breath, body and mind as a result of the exercises they are performing.

It is equally important to finish each play of breath by having the children observe the return to their natural breath when the exercise is complete. In this way they will be able to observe any changes that occur as a result of the exercise and they can assess how they feel about the outcome.

Each play of breath description represents one round of the exercise. It is up to the teacher to gauge how many rounds or how long the children will perform each play of breath. I would always recommend starting off slowly and simply, gradually building the awareness, strength and stamina of the children.

Pronunciation guide to Sanskrit words is available on knower.ca

Keep it simple and enjoy!

## Awareness of the Movement of Breath
## प्राण चिन्तन प्राणायाम Prān Chintan Prānāyām

**Pronunciation**: *prān*, the *ā* is pronounced as in "on;" *chintan*, the *i* is pronounced as in "chin," the *a* is pronounced as "hum;" *prānāyām*, the *ā* is pronounced as in "on"

**Meaning**: प्राण *prān* is that which moves the breath in and moves the breath out. चिन्तन *chintan* means awareness. The meaning of *prān chintan* is awareness of the movement of breath. *Prān chintan* is a direct method of getting connected to the Knower. प्राणायाम *prānāyām* means channelling the power that moves the breath.

**Benefits**: This exercise is about watching the movement of breath, and paying attention to where the breath starts, and where the breath stops. It rejuvenates the inner system of the child making him or her calm, clear and balanced.

Please remind the children not to exert. This exercise is about watching and discovering the pattern and rhythm of their own unique system. It is also a marvellous exercise to prepare the mind and body for meditation.

**How to do it**: Have the children breathe normally through their nose. Ask them to pay attention to their breathing in and breathing out.

You can ask them to observe how long it takes for them to breathe out through their nose. For fun they can count in their mind or use their fingers to measure the timing of their exhalation.

When the children feel that their exhalation is complete and they are ready to inhale, ask them to pay attention to the change in direction, from exhalation to inhalation. They will observe that when the breath changes direction there is a pause. Ask them to pay attention to, and hold, that pause for a second or two.

The children can observe the movement of their breath as they slowly breathe in, pause, breathe out, pause, and so forth. As they observe the pattern of their breathing in this exercise, they can pay attention to the one who is watching the movement of their breath. The one who is watching is their own Self, the Knower.

When the exercise is complete they can watch as their breath returns to its natural pattern, and note how they feel as a result.

# Abdominal Breathing
# अधम प्राणायाम Adham Prānāyām

**Pronunciation**: *adham*, the *a* is pronounced as in "hum;" *prānāyām*, the *ā* is pronounced as in "on"

**Meaning**: In Sanskrit the word अधम *adham* means low. प्राणायाम *prānāyām* means channelling the power that moves the breath.

**Benefits**: This exercise involves breathing from the abdominal or tummy area. Abdominal breathing deepens the breath, which guides the children to use their full breath most efficiently. It also calms and stabilizes their disposition. This full yogic breathing technique forms the foundation of many pranayama exercises.

**How to do it**: Before they begin, have the children pay attention to the rising and falling of their natural breath. Ask them to place their fingers on the area where they feel their breath rise and fall. Most likely the children will place their fingers on their chest.

Now ask the children to place their fingers on their tummy. Tell them that their fingers are the destination point to where they want to guide their breath.

Ask them to breathe in and gently guide their breath to reach their fingers. When their breath reaches their fingers, their tummy will puff up. Then they can pause for a second or two.

Ask them to breathe out slowly and watch as their fingers, on their tummy, go down. Then they can pause for a second or two.

As they become more comfortable with this exercise, they can make their breaths slower and deeper.

When the children have finished this play of breath they can watch as their natural rhythm of breathing returns. You can ask them how they feel after completing this exercise.

# Balanced Breathing
# सम-वृत्ति प्राणायाम Sam-Vritti Prānāyām

**Pronunciation**: *sam*, the *a* sound is pronounced as in "hum;" *vritti*, the *i* is pronounced as in "chin;" *prānāyām*, the *ā* is pronounced as in "on"

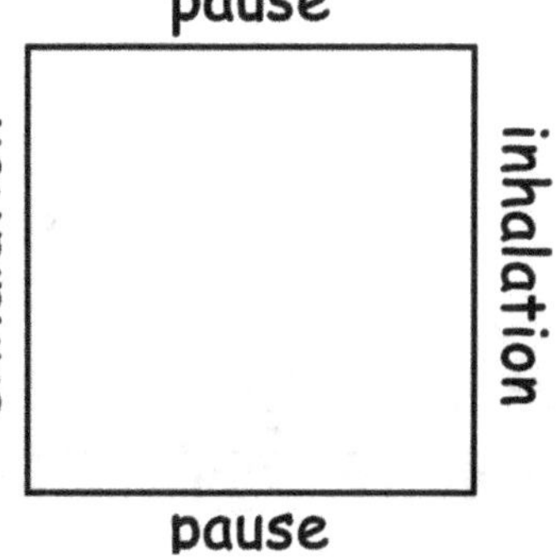


**Meaning**: सम *sam* means balanced or the same, and वृत्ति *vritti* means whirlpool; it refers to the fluctuations of the mind. प्राणायाम *prānāyām* means channelling the power that moves the breath.

**Benefits**: Balanced Breathing is a soothing, calming and centring practice, which helps to calm the mind as it reduces stress and anxiety.

In this exercise the children will try to make the inhalation, pause, exhalation, pause, of equal length. They can count mentally or with their fingers. Please have them start off slowly, easily and comfortably. Over time they can build their capacity.

This Balanced Breathing exercise is sometimes likened to the shape of a square. In a square all the sides are equal. The children can inhale, pause, exhale, pause...while they make a square either in their mind or draw a square in the air using their finger.

**Please note**: Holding the breath on the inhalation is easier than on the exhalation.

**How to do it**: Have the children bring their awareness to their natural breath and observe their breathing in and breathing out.

Ask the children to count to two as they comfortably inhale.

When they reach the count of two at the end of their inhalation, ask them to try to hold their breath comfortably to the same count of two. There should be no strain involved.

Then ask them to try to breathe out to the same count of two. Again there should be no strain involved.

Ask them to try to hold their exhalation to the same count of two if they can.

When the exercise is complete they can watch as their breath returns to its natural pattern. You can ask them how they feel.

## Alternate Nostril Breathing
## अनुलोम-विलोम प्राणायाम Anulom-Vilom Prānāyām

**Pronunciation**: *anulom*, the *a* is pronounced as in "hum," the *u* is pronounced as in "full" and the *o* is pronounced as in "home;" *vilom*, the *i* is pronounced as in "chin," the *o* is pronounced as in "home;" *prānāyām*, the *ā* is pronounced as in "on"

**Meaning**: In Sanskrit the word अनुलोम *anulom* means "to go with the grain," and विलोम *vilom* means "to go against the grain." So *anulom* is the opposite to *vilom*, and *vilom* is opposite to *anulom*. प्राणायाम *prānāyām* means channelling the power that moves the breath.

**Benefits**: This pranayama forms the foundation of other breathing exercises. This exercise balances the nervous system, focuses the mind and improves concentration. It is said to maintain body temperature and fight colds.

**How to do it**: Have the children sit in a relaxed and comfortable position, and observe their natural breathing.

Ask them to block their right nostril with their right thumb, breathe in through their left nostril and then pause for a second or two.

Then ask them to release their right nostril and block their left nostril with one of their fingers. Ask them to breathe out through the right nostril and then pause for a second or two.

With their left nostril still blocked, ask them to breathe in through their right nostril and pause for a second or two.

Have them release their left nostril and block their right nostril with one of their fingers. Ask them to breathe out through their left nostril and then pause for a second or two.

This is one round of alternate nostril breathing, which can be repeated.

**Simply put**:

- breathe in through the left nostril,
- pause,
- breathe out through the right nostril,
- pause,
- breathe in through the right nostril,
- pause,
- breathe out through the left nostril,
- pause.

When they are finished, have them take some time to allow their breath to return to normal and observe the changes to their breath and mind.

# Warming Breath
# सूर्य भेदि प्राणायाम Sūrya Bhedi Prānāyām

**Pronunciation**: *sūrya*, the *ū* is pronounced as in "hoop," the *a* is pronounced as in "hum;" *bhedi*, the *e* is pronounced as in "hay," the *i* is pronounced as in "chin;" *prānāyām*, the *ā* is pronounced as in "on"

**Meaning**: सूर्य *surya* in Sanskrit means the sun and भेदि *bhedi* means piercing or breaking through. प्राणायाम *pranayam* means channelling the power that moves the breath.

**Benefits**: This exercise provides energy and warmth to the body and is said to improve digestion.

**How to do it**: Ask the children to sit quietly and comfortably and watch their natural breath.

Ask the children to close their left nostril; they can do so with their thumb or fingers. Slowly and gently they can inhale through their right nostril filling up their lungs.

Ask them to pause by holding their breath for a few seconds, as long as they feel comfortable.

Then they can close their right nostril and exhale slowly and easily.

This is one round of Warming Breath. You can have the children repeat the round a few times if you like.

When the exercise is complete, the children can watch as their natural breathing pattern returns. You can ask them if they feel a bit warmer.

# Victory Breath or Ocean Breath
## उज्जायी प्राणायाम Ujjayī Prānāyām

**Pronunciation**: *ujjayī*, the *u* is pronounced as in "full," the *a* is pronounced as in "hum," the *ī* is pronounced as in "tea;" *prānāyām*, the *ā* is pronounced as in "on"

**Meaning**: उज्जायी *ujjayī* means victory or the victorious one, and so this exercise is called victory breath. प्राणायाम *prānāyām* means channelling the power that moves the breath.

The sound that is made while performing this pranayama is likened to the sound of the ocean and so this exercise also goes by the name "ocean breath."

**Benefits**: This pranayama helps to calm the mind and warm the body.

**How to do it**: To warm up, ask the children to breathe in through their nose, taking a long, slow, deep breath, pause and slowly breathe out fully.

They can begin by breathing in with both nostrils feeling the intake of air at the back of their throat while keeping their mouth closed. This inhalation creates a soft hissing sound that is likened to the sound of the ocean.

They can hold their breath for a second or two.

Ask the children to close their right nostril and slowly breathe out from their left nostril.

This is one round of Victory Breath.

When the exercise is complete, the children can watch as their breath returns to its natural rhythm.

# Cooling Breath शीतली प्राणायाम Shītalī Prānāyām

**Pronunciation**: *shītalī*, the *ī* is pronounced as in "tea," the *a* is pronounced as in "hum;" *pranayam*, the *ā* is pronounced as in "on"

**Meaning**: शीतली *shītalī* means cooling in Sanskrit and प्राणायाम *prānāyām* means channelling the power that moves the breath.

**Benefits**: This exercise will cool and soothe the body and calm the mind, as well as reduce stress, anger and anxiety.

**How to do it**: Have the children sit comfortably and watch their natural breath. Then ask them to take a deep breath in and exhale fully in preparation for this exercise.

Ask the children to stick out their tongue. Then ask if they can roll their tongue like a tube or straw. (The action of pulling air through the tongue creates a cooling effect on the body.)

If any of the children are unable to roll their tongue you can ask them to purse their lips, making a small "O" shape with their lips. (This is called *Shītkarī Prānāyām* and it means the breathing technique that produces a hissing sound.)

Have the children breathe in through their tube-shaped tongue or through the small "O" shape of their lips. As the air is indrawn the air will make a soft hissing sound.

When the inhalation is complete they can bring their tongue back into their mouth or close their lips and exhale through their nose.

This is one round of Cooling Breath.

When the exercise is complete, the children can watch as their natural breath returns. You can ask them if they feel a bit cooler.

# Shining Forehead
## कपालभाति प्राणायाम Kapālbhāti Prānāyām

**Pronunciation**: *kapālbhāti*, the *a* is pronounced as in "hum," the *ā* is pronounced as in "on," the *i* is pronounced as in "chin;" *pranāyām*, the *ā* is pronounced as in "on"

**Meaning**: The word कपालभाति *kapālbhāti* comes from two Sanskrit words: कपाल *kapāl* means the skull or head; भाति *bhāti* means lighting or illuminating. प्राणायाम *prānāyām* means channelling the power that moves the breath.

**Benefits**: This play of breath improves blood circulation, which adds radiance to the face. It energizes the nervous system while calming and uplifting the mind.

**How to do it**: Have the children sit comfortably and watch their natural breath. They can try two or three deep inhalations and exhalations in preparation for this exercise.

Ask them to inhale deeply into their tummy, and watch as their tummy puffs up a bit. They can pause for a second or two before exhaling.

The emphasis in this exercise is on the exhalation. When the children exhale through the nose, it should be done energetically, but not with any force.

As they exhale their tummy will be drawn inward as if the air is being pushed out of their tummy.

If the children complete a few rounds, they will notice that the inhalations are passive, easy and natural, and happen as a result of the energetic exhalations.

When they have completed this play of breath they can watch as their breath returns to its natural flow.

# Bellows Breath
## भस्त्रिका प्राणायाम Bhastrikā Prānāyām

**Pronunciation**: *bhastrikā*, the *a* is pronounced as in "hum," the *i* is pronounced as in "chin," the *ā* is pronounced as in "on;" *prānāyām*, the *ā* is pronounced as in "on"

**Meaning**: In Sanskrit भस्त्रिका *bhastrikā* means bellows—a device used for producing a strong current of air to fan a fire. So *bhastrikā prānāyām* means breathing like a bellows. प्राणायाम *prānāyām* means channelling the power that moves the breath.

**Benefits**: This nourishing exercise brings about balance, enhances the digestive capabilities and creates heat in the body. It also strengthens the lungs and calms the mind.

**How to do it**: Have the children sit comfortably and watch their natural breath.

To begin this exercise, ask the children to take a long deep breath in through their nose, filling their lungs as much as they can.

Then ask them to breathe out, through their nose, all the air they just inhaled. Then pause for a second or two.

The children should pay attention, that the length and strength of the inhalation should match the length and strength of the exhalation.

When the exercise is complete have the children observe their breath returning to its natural rhythm.

**It is important to note** that Bellows Breath can be performed slowly or rapidly. The children can begin slowly and increase the pace of the exercise, but they should never force their breath.

# Humming Bee भ्रमरी प्राणायाम Bhramarī Prānāyām

**Pronunciation**: *bhramarī*, the *a* sound is pronounced as in "hum," the *ī* is pronounced as in "tea;" *prānāyām*, the *ā* is pronounced as in "on"

**Meaning**: भ्रमरी *bhramarī* is the Sanskrit word for a type of bee found in India. This pranayama is called *bhramarī* because when the breath is exhaled, the sound produced is likened to the humming of a bee. प्राणायाम *prānāyām* means channelling the power that moves the breath.

**Benefits**: This exercise is great for calming the mind and freeing it from agitation, frustration, anxiety and anger. It is also good for insomnia.

**How to do it**: Have the children sit comfortably and watch their breath as they relax and breathe normally.

Ask them to take a deep breath in through their nose and pause for a second or two.

Ask the children to exhale slowly and steadily through their nose making a sweet melodious humming sound like a bee hovering over a flower. Ask if they can try to keep their humming sound at the same continuous pitch, tone or sound level.

The children should also try to match the timing of their inhalation with their exhalation.

This is one round of Humming Bee.

When the exercise is complete, let their breath return to its natural rhythm and ask them to observe the effect of this exercise.

# Chanting Breath उद्गीथ प्राणायाम Udgīth Prānāyām

**Pronunciation**: *udgīth*, the *u* is pronounced as in "full," the *ī* is pronounced as in "tea," the *th* at the end of the word is an aspirated *t* sound as in "talk;" *prānāyām*, the *ā* is pronounced as in "on"

**Meaning**: उद्गीथ *udgīth* means chanting and प्राणायाम *prānāyām* means channelling the power that moves the breath.

**Benefits**: This play of breath calms the mind while it relieves tension and anxiety.

**How to do it**: Have the children sit comfortably while watching the natural rhythm of their own breathing.

Ask them to breathe in slowly and deeply through their nose and then pause for a second or two.

As they exhale slowly, ask them to chant a mantra such as *Om* or *Hum*. In this exercise the emphasis is on breathing out the sound "*mmmm*."

Each chanting exhalation represents one round of this exercise and can easily be repeated. It is also a very nice lead-in to meditation.

When the exercise is complete the children can quietly observe their natural breath returning.

# The Sound of Om प्रणव प्राणायाम Pranav Prānāyām

**Pronunciation**: *pranav*, the *a* is pronounced as in "hum," *prānāyām*, the *ā* is pronounced as in "on"

**Meaning**: प्रणव *pranav* refers to the syllable *Om* and प्राणायाम *prānāyām* means channelling the power that moves the breath.

**Benefits**: This exercise is said to reduce stress while providing peace and steadiness to the mind. It is great as a lead-in to meditation.

**How to do it**: Have the children sit comfortably and breathe normally through their nose as they watch the flow of their natural breath, and pay attention to their own rhythm and movement.

While focusing on their own breathing pattern—inhalation, pause, exhalation, pause—the children can breath the sound *Om* in their minds.

**Variation**: As an alternative to focusing on the sound of *Om*, each child can choose a mantra or sound that makes them feel good.

# King of Pranayama
## केवल कुम्भक प्राणायाम Keval Kumbhak Prānāyām

**Pronunciation**: *keval*, the *e* is pronounced as in "hay," the *a* is pronounced as in "hum;" *kumbhak*, the *u* is pronounced as in "full," the *a* is pronounced as in "hum;" *prānāyām*, the *ā* is pronounced as in "on"

**Meaning**: केवल *keval* means only or alone, and कुम्भक *kumbhak* means to pause. *Keval kumbhak* is not simply holding the breath; *keval kumbhak* is the pause that happens when the *prān* changes direction from inhaling to exhaling, and from exhaling to inhaling. प्राणायाम *prānāyām* means channelling the power that moves the breath.

**Benefits**: When this exercise is held, the children should try to watch the space between the inhalation and the exhalation. Their watching will turn into knowing that the one who is watching is the one who is always there. When the breath resumes they will come to see that it is the breath that comes and goes, but the watcher of the breath is always there.

In fact, King of Pranayama is technically not a pranayama exercise because it has nothing to do with the movement of breath—neither breathing in nor breathing out. When this exercise is performed, the children will not be attending the movement of breath, because there is none. The children will be watching only (*keval*) the pause (*kumbhak*) between the in breath and the out breath, or between the out breath and the in breath.

It is said that King of Pranayama (*keval kumbhak*) is the fourth state of consciousness, the Knower state of the Self.

**How to do it**: It is simple to perform initially. However, it is a very refined and subtle exercise that is to be done with effortless ease.

Have the children sit comfortably and at ease. Ask them to watch the movement of their breath as they breathe in and breathe out.

At some point you can ask the children to either decide for themselves when to pause the breath, or you can make a game of it and ask the children to pause and retain their breath when you say the word "*kumbhak*." Children can observe at what point *kumbhak* happens for each of them—whether it was on the inhalation or the exhalation, and how it feels to observe the pause.

Holding the pause (*kumbhak*) should be natural and easy. Absolutely never force it. Through practice, holding the pause becomes more and more effortless and refined. It can be performed either on the in breath or the out breath. Children can experiment with what feels most comfortable to them.

This play of breath is a fabulous lead-in to meditation. Through the practice of this exercise the mind becomes more relaxed, focused, at ease and in tune with the space of the Knower.

# Chapter 3

# The Play of Sound, Mantra

Just because the mind is busy creating thoughts, that doesn't mean you have to listen to them. The mind has the power to create thought and you have the power to create *mantr*...
(Swami Shyam, 1994, *Vision of Oneness*, p 203)

Mantra is a Sanskrit word. The root word *man* means mind and the suffix *tra* means instrument of release or freedom. Therefore, the meaning of mantra is that it is an instrument that releases the mind from the binding effects of thoughts, ideas and conclusions. Mantra is an instrument of freedom.

Sound is very powerful. Every sound is unique in its vibration, pitch, frequency, resonance, duration and rhythm. You must have experienced the power of music. It can evoke all manner of feelings, from sadness and tears to triumph and exultation. I remember seeing a commercial on television many years ago. An opera singer sustained a particular note, and in so doing, shattered a crystal glass. It was amazing. The commercial demonstrated the power of sound to its viewers. In the same way, repeating a mantra in meditation can shatter the power that binds you to thoughts of uneasiness.

Most often we think of sound as that which is only audible to the ears. However, sound uttered in the mind as thoughts and memories carry their own subtle power and influence. Mantra uses the subtle aspect of sound and meaning to transform thoughts of unease to those of peace, joy and freedom. The ancient yogis heard the sound of the Knower in meditation and presented these sounds to the world as mantras.

In meditation, mantras are helpful tools used to engage the mind in thoughts of peace, love, unity and freedom. In this way negative thoughts that create uneasiness, worry and anxiety don't easily arise. When the mind is focused on positivity, then there is little or no room left for negativity.

Sound and meaning go hand in hand when introducing Sanskrit mantras. Revealing the meaning of a mantra gives children the opportunity to become acquainted with its sound and ponder its meaning.

Children learn through repetition. You can introduce a Sanskrit mantra to your class by repeating aloud its proper pronunciation. (Please see the pronunciation guide provided with each mantra.) The children can chime in to the rhythm of your repetition as the whole class joins their voices to chant or echo the mantra. Gradually you can shift the volume from audible to whispering and finally you can ask them to repeat the mantra quietly inside their minds. If they can attend the meaning while repeating the mantra that would be wonderful.

There is a definite science behind the selection and use of mantras. The power of mantra is subtle and can influence the mood and mind of the child. Different sounds, words and meanings produce different results, and influence the mind in different ways. Therefore, selecting mantras that carry positivity, peace, delight and the sense of well-being is most essential.

When a mantra is repeated, its meaning is also experienced. For example if a word or thought carries a painful meaning then pain will be the result, if it carries a joyful meaning then joy will be the result.

Mantras can be a single sound, a word or group of words. Mantras are also specific songs or poems. In this chapter I have included simple mantras that are a single word or a few words. Any word or sound repeated with meaning and intent for the betterment of the person can be considered a mantra. Therefore, mantras can be both contemporary and ancient and specific to the cultural conditions of the children.

Traditional Sanskrit mantras have passed the test of time. They have been handed down from teacher to student for millennia. When practicing traditional mantras it is known what the outcome will be—peace, freedom, happiness, detachment, clarity, love and highest awareness, to name a few. That is why selecting traditional Sanskrit mantras is always a great idea.

On the other hand, you should feel free to experiment with your students by creating your own mantras with sounds and words that represent qualities the children would like to possess. You might like to try out different mantras with your class and later discuss how the chosen mantra made them feel. In this way, children can learn about choice and how to play with sound.

It is important that children find their own stride and rhythm when repeating a mantra. They should never feel forced. They should like the sound and aspire to the meaning of the mantra they have selected to repeat.

When a mantra, as well as its meaning, is repeated in meditation, the mind becomes absorbed in its sound, meaning and fragrance. The children will then start to experience the qualities and merits of that mantra and as a result they will begin to think and feel much, much better.

Use your skill and care when selecting mantras for children. I have provided a selection of traditional Sanskrit mantras for you to try out with your class. Included with the listed mantras is a pronunciation guide as well as a description of each mantra's meaning.

Feel free to experiment with your own mantras.

Enjoy!

P.S. To enhance "mantra meditation" the use of a mala is a great tactile activity to focus and concentrate the minds of children in meditation. (see Mala in The Play of Action, Karma Yoga)

# Mantras

The original Sanskrit verses were devised and composed on the basis of the eternal rhythm....By singing the verses with the proper pronunciation...one's individual, bound mind is released from the grip and power of the senses...
(Swami Shyam, 1985, *Bhagavad Gita: The Most Precise and Comprehensive Rendering*, page 21)

The correct pronunciation of Sanskrit mantras is important, because the meaning is hidden within the sound. Using the correct pronunciation is like playing an instrument that has been tuned properly. When children repeat the mantra with proper pronunciation the resonance of the ancient, eternal sound and its meaning calms the fidgety consciousness of the mind, allowing it to relax into the peace of its own source or true home, the unchanging Knower.

When a mantra ends with the sound *m* it is helpful to elongate the *m* sound because the resonance of *mmmm...* carries the mind to its source, the Knower.

A pronunciation guide for each Sanskrit mantra is available on knower.ca

## Amaram Hum Madhuram Hum अमरम् हं मधुरम् हं

**Pronunciation**: *amaram*, the *a* is pronounced as in "hum;" *madhuram*, the *a* is pronounced as in "hum," the *u* is pronounced as "full," the *dh* represents a single Devanagari* letter which has no English equivalent. Both the *d* and *h* are pronounced simultaneously to create a single unbroken sound, as in the words "gold hoop;" the Sanskrit *dhu* in *madhuram* closely resembles the quickly pronounced, unified *dhoo* sound as in "gold hoop." The sound *m* as the final consonant of "hum" should be elongated as *mmmm…* to carry the mind to the Knower.

**Meaning and Benefits**: This mantra is a revelation. It is the sound from the source, the voice of the Knower that was revealed to my teacher, Swami Shyam. It means "I am immortal, I am blissful." It is a very beautiful mantra that guides whoever repeats it to their own true Self, the Knower. *Amaram Hum* I am immortal, *Madhuram Hum* I am Blissful.

## Om or Aum ॐ or ओम

**Pronunciation**: *om*, the *o* is pronounced as in "home." The sound *m* as the final consonant of "hum" should be elongated as *mmmm…* to carry the mind to the Knower. When reciting *Om* there should be equal emphasis on both parts of the mantra—*O* or *Au* and *m*.

**Meaning and Benefits**: *Om* is the essential building block upon which all sounds are based. *Om* produces a state of peace, clarity and highest awareness. It is the sound of the universe and of peace. The sound *Om* is universally used as a meditation mantra. It is said that within the sound *Om* or *Aum* is the entire Devanagari alphabet*—beginning with the first letter, the vowel "a," and ending with the last, the consonant "m." It is the Devanagri version of A-Z. Therefore, the mantra *Om* is said to include all words.

---

* The Sanskrit language is written using the Devanagari alphabet.

# Om Shānti ॐ शान्ति

**Pronunciation**: *om*, the *o* is pronounced as in "home." The sound *m* as the final consonant of "hum" should be elongated as *mmmm...* to carry the mind to the Knower. *Shānti*, the *ā* is pronounced as in "on," the *i* is pronounced as in "chin"

**Meaning and Benefits**: The sound *Om* represents the whole of manifestation, while *Shānti* means peace, restfulness, calmness, tranquility or bliss. Together *Om Shānti* is the invocation of peace on earth, peace for all beings and peace for the whole.

Often this mantra is repeated as *Om Shānti Shānti Shānti* at the end of a longer poem or mantra, indicating its conclusion. The sound *Om Shānti Shānti Shānti* resonates with the sense of peace within and without.

# Hum हं

**Pronunciation**: *hum*, is pronounced as it is in English. The sound *m* as the final consonant of "hum" should be elongated as *mmmm...* to carry the mind to the Knower.

**Meaning and Benefits**: *Hum* means "I as That." It is described as the sound of the space that is before the utterance "I." It represents the original space that stands by itself.

# So Hum सो हं

**Pronunciation**: *so*, is pronounced as it is in English, *hum*, is pronounced as it is in English. The sound *m* as the final consonant of "hum" should be elongated as *mmmm...* to carry the mind to the Knower.

**Meaning and Benefits**: *So Hum* is a reflection of the sound of the breath. Breathing in *So*, meaning "I am," and breathing out *Hum*, meaning "I as That." *So Hum* means "I am That." This mantra lends itself well to repetition in conjunction with pranayama. It aligns the mind with the unchanging Knower. When repeated, it brings a sense of calm and ease to the mind.

## Rām राम

**Pronunciation**: *rām*, the *ā* is pronounced as in "on." The sound *m* as the final consonant of "hum" should be elongated as *mmmm...* to carry the mind to the Knower.

**Meaning and Benefits**: *Rām* exemplifies the achievement of perfection and virtue. When repeating the mantra *Rām* you can add a short "a" at the end to make it easier to repeat. *RāmaRāmaRāmaRām...* The mantra *Rām* is said to enhance self-esteem, will power and mental strength, while attracting success and happiness.

## Jai Rām Shrī Rām जय राम श्री राम

**Pronunciation**: *jai*, the *ai* is pronounced somewhere between "I" and "jay," there is no English equivalent; *rām*, the *ā* is pronounced as in "on." The sound *m* as the final consonant of "hum" should be elongated as *mmmm...* to carry the mind to the Knower. *Shrī*, the *ī* is pronounced as in "tea;" *rām*, the *ā* is pronounced as in "on." The sound *m* as the final consonant of "hum" should be elongated as *mmmm...* to carry the mind to the Knower.

**Meaning and Benefits**: *Jai* mean victory, *Rām* represents perfection and virtue and *Shrī* is a title of respect. This mantra celebrates the victory of good over evil. It is often repeated as,
*Jai Rām Shrī Rām Jai Jai Rām,*
*Jai Rām Shrī Rām Jai Jai Rām.*

# Shiv शिव

**Pronunciation**: *shiv*, the *i* is pronounced as in "chin"

**Meaning and Benefits**: The mantra *Shiv* is said to bring the happiness that comes from the sense of unity and harmony with all of creation, yet remains undisturbed by change and disappearance. Thus, this mantra brings about inner happiness and detachment. When repeating the mantra *Shiv* you can add a short *a* at the end to make it easier to repeat. *ShivaShivaShivaShiv...*

# Shyām श्याम

**Pronunciation**: *shyām*, the sound of *sh* blends with the consonant sound of *y* as in "yellow" to form a single consonant sound of *shy* (not like the English word "shy" where y is a vowel). The sound *shy* has no English equivalent, the *ā* is pronounced as in "on."

**Meaning and Benefits**: The mantra *Shyām* represents the blue-black space that is untouched by the world of things and forms. It is the unchanging Knower space, the place from where manifestation springs. By repeating the mantra *Shyām*, awareness of the Knower is enhanced and the power of observation strengthened. When repeating the mantra *Shyām* you can add a short *a* at the end to make it easier to repeat. *ShyāmaShyāmaShyāmaShyām...*

# Hare Krishna Hare Rām हरे कृष्ण हरे राम

**Pronunciation**: *hare*, the *a* is pronounced as in "hum," the *e* is pronounced as in "hay;" *Krishna*, the *i* is pronounced as in "chin," the *a* is pronounced as in "hum;" *hare*, the *a* is pronounced as in "hum," the *e* is pronounced as in "hay;" *rām*, the *ā* is pronounced as in "on." The sound *m* as the final consonant of "hum" should be elongated as *mmmm...* to carry the mind to the Knower.

**Meaning and Benefits**: In Sanskrit *Hare* means the ultimate energy, *Krishna* means black or dark in colour and *Rām* means perfection. This mantra, known as the Great Mantra, celebrates liberation from bondage and is recited to promote highest awareness. It found its way into popular culture when George Harrison wrote the song "My Sweet Lord."

*Hare Krishna Hare Krishna, Krishna Krishna, Hare Hare*
*Hare Rām Hare Rām, Rām Rām, Hare Hare*

# Om Rām Shiv Shyām ॐ राम शिव श्याम

**Pronunciation**: *om*, the *o* is pronounced as in "home." The sound *m* as the final consonant of "hum" should be elongated as *mmmm*... to carry the mind to the Knower. *Rām*, the *ā* is pronounced as in "on." The sound *m* as the final consonant of "hum" should be elongated as *mmmm*... to carry the mind to the Knower. *Shiv*, the *i* is pronounced as in "chin," *Shyām*, the sound of *sh* blends with the consonant sound of *y* as in "yellow" to form a single consonant sound of *shy* (not like the English word "shy" where y is a vowel). The sound *shy* has no English equivalent, the *ā* is pronounced as in "on."

**Meaning and Benefits**: This mantra is a lovely combination of peace, compassion, bliss and detachment.

## Mantras of your own choosing.

Have the children play and experiment with sounds, words and phrases that make them feel good about themselves and enhance the sense of peace, freedom, confidence and delight, such as "Pure, Free, Forever" or "Peace, Love, Peace, Love."

You can also choose mantras from the children's cultural heritage. For example, you can choose the English word "peace" and find out its translation in the heritage language of the children in your class. For example, French-paix, Hindi-shanti, Hebrew-shalom, Spanish-paz, etc.

# Chapter 4

# The Play of Body, Hatha Yoga

Begin at the beginning...and go on till you come to the end: then stop. (Lewis Carroll, 1865, *Alice in Wonderland*)

The purpose of this chapter is to familiarize the children with their body and provide focus for their mind. This focus will help them relax, settle down and have fun, while directing their energy towards meditation. Hatha yoga poses are specifically designed body movements that encourage the children's consciousness to be aligned with the Knower.

The word "hatha" comes from two Sanskrit words, "ha" meaning the sun, and "tha" meaning the moon. It represents the opposing energies in a human being. Hatha also means efforts. The meaning of the word "yoga" is union. Hatha yoga refers to the practice and efforts of uniting the opposing energies of a human being—the energy of the unchanging Knower as represented by the sun, and the energy of the changing mind and body as represented by the moon.

Through practicing hatha yoga a state of balance is achieved. It is important to note that hatha yoga poses go hand in hand with the play of breath, pranayama. It is said that the breath completes the physical pose.

Through hatha yoga the children build concentration, memory, focus and body-mind coordination skills, which help them create and maintain a peaceful and calm presence. It enhances flexibility, balance and strength in their body and attentiveness in their mind, which can help them cope with challenging situations. The exercises utilize the children's body and mind for the growth and development of outer strength and inner peace.

Children should never feel that they are struggling to do a pose. Encourage children to do the poses correctly but don't force physical perfection, because the purpose of hatha yoga is to enjoy, relax and settle the body and mind so that the meditative state can happen easily. Please remember to encourage the children to breathe during their poses. Watching the breath while doing hatha yoga poses inspires a greater sense of focus, interest and concentration.

The word *āsan* means pose or posture in Sanskrit. All the names of the poses have the word *āsan* at the end indicating they are poses. Teachers can call the poses by their English names or by their original Sanskrit names, both are provided. Learning a few Sanskrit words can be fun and empowering to children.

Just to keep the class interesting, teachers can have the children partner up with one or more friends to do poses. Simple partnering encourages cooperation and builds problem-solving skills. For example the children can be trees in the forest while they are all standing in the tree pose or they can sit back-to-back while performing some sitting poses. Practicing hatha yoga with partners can help keep their focus on the pose at hand while having fun with their friends.

**Please remember** to have drinking water available. Keeping the body hydrated is important. Drinking water cools down the physical and mental system of the child.

Keep it simple and have fun.

I have included a variety of hatha yoga poses to complement the stories and enhance the meditation experience. Teachers should feel free to introduce and adapt the poses to suit the needs, ages and abilities of their students.

Pronunciation guide to Sanskrit words is available on knower.ca

> Whatever is worth doing is worth doing well.
> (Lewis Carroll, 1865, *Alice In Wonderland*)

Enjoy!

# Hatha Yoga Poses

## Mountain Pose ताड़ासन Tādāsan

**Pronunciation**: *tādāsan*, the *ā* is pronounced as in "on," the *a* is pronounced as in "hum"

**Meaning**: In Sanskrit ताड़ *tād* means mountain and आसन *āsan* means pose.

**Benefits**: This standing pose is grounding for children as they cultivate the strength, stillness and power of a mountain. It helps stretch their entire body, improve their balance and focus their concentration.

**How to do it**: Ask the children to stand with both feet facing forward, hip-width apart, and arms by their sides. Have them stand tall, stretch out their back, puff out their chest and keep their shoulders relaxed.

Have the children flex their toes up and down, while they let their body gently rock back and forth a few times as they find their balance.

Ask them to bend their elbows, bring their palms together towards their chest, and hold for one or two breaths before lowering their arms.

If the children can remember to pay attention to their breath, that would be great!

# Tree Pose वृक्षासन Vrikshāsan

**Pronunciation**: *vrikshāsan*, the *i* is pronounced as in "chin," the *ā* is pronounced as in "on," the *a* is pronounced as in "hum"

**Meaning**: In Sanskrit वृक्ष *vriksh* means tree and आसन *āsan* means pose.

**Benefits**: This standing pose helps improve balance, alertness, concentration and mental clarity.

**How to do it**: Have the children start by standing straight, feet hip-width apart, as in the mountain pose, and gently observe their breath.

As they breathe out, have them slowly raise one foot and place the sole of this foot, toes pointing down, as high as is comfortable on the inner thigh of the stationary leg.

Ask them to slowly stretch their arms above their head and bring their palms together. They will observe how their balance becomes steady and their alignment refined.

If they can remember to observe their breath that would be great!

**A hint for keeping balance**: Ask the children to pick a point in front of them to stare at. Focusing on one point will help them with their balance.

They should repeat this on the other leg.

# Forward-Fold Pose उत्तानासन Uttānāsan

**Pronunciation**: *uttānāsan*, the *u* is pronounced as in "full," the *ā* is pronounced as in "on," the *a* is pronounced as in "hum"

**Meaning**: In Sanskrit उत *ut* means intense, तान *tān* means stretch and आसन *āsan* means pose.

**Benefits**: This pose gives flexibility to the hips, strengthens the knees and spine, stretches the legs and improves posture and alignment. It also eases tension in the back, shoulders and neck. This pose is said to be rejuvenating and revitalizing.

**How to do it**: Have the children start by standing straight, feet hip-width apart, as in the mountain pose, and gently observe their breath.

As they breathe out, they can slowly bend forward from the hips, trying to keep their legs straight, if they can.

With their head relaxed and facing downward, the children can try to touch their fingertips, or even their palms, on the floor.

They can hold the position for a breath or two.

Then they can breathe in, and slowly come back to the standing position.

# Equestrian Pose
# अश्व सञ्चलनासन Ashwa Sanchalanāsan

**Pronunciation**: *ashwa sanchalanāsan*, the *a* is pronounced as in "hum," the *ā* is pronounced as in "on"

**Meaning**: In Sanskrit the word अश्व *ashwa* means horse, सञ्चलन *sanchalan* means stepping movement and आसन *āsan* means pose.

**Benefits**: This lunge pose helps improve balance as it stretches the leg muscles, opens the hips and lengthens the spine. It is said to increase willpower, courage, determination and digestion.

Most often this pose follows the forward-fold pose, when performing the Sun Salutation Poses.

**How to do it**: Have the children bend        forward as if from the forward fold-pose, placing their palms on the floor.

Ask them to breathe in and extend one leg back as far as is comfortable, keeping that knee straight.

As they do this, they will bend the knee of the forward leg, keeping the forward foot in the same position. They should pay attention to place their bent knee directly above the ankle.

With their arms on either side of the forward leg, fingers touching the floor, ask them to arch their back and tilt their head back.

They can hold the pose for a breath or two.

**A hint for keeping balance**: Ask the children to pick a point in front of them to stare at. Focusing on one point will help them with their balance.

# Raised Hands Pose ऊर्ध्व हास्तासन Ūrdhva Hāstāsan

**Pronunciation**: *ūrdhva hāstāsan*, the *ū* is pronounced as in "hoop," the *ā* is pronounced as in "on," the *a* is pronounced as in "hum"

**Meaning**: In Sanskrit ऊर्ध्व *ūrdhva* means upward, हास्त *hāst* means hands and आसन *āsan* means pose.

**Benefits**: This pose helps to extend the upper body as it strengthens the arms and shoulders. This pose is said to rejuvenate, energize and relieve anxiety.

**How to do it**: Have the children start by standing straight, feet hip-width apart, as in the mountain pose, arms by their sides. Ask them to observe their breath before beginning the pose.

Ask the children to breathe in and slowly raise their straight arms forward, sweeping them above their head. They should try to keep their shoulders and neck relaxed.

As they raise their arms they can expand their chest and gently tilt their body backward, pushing their hips forward and engaging the front of their thighs.

Hold for a breath or two.

# Downward-Facing Dog Pose
# अधोमुखश्वानासन Adho Mukh Shwānāsan

**Pronunciation**: *adho mukh shwānāsan*, the *a* is pronounced as in "hum," the *o* is pronounced as in "home," the *u* is pronounced as in "full," the *ā* is pronounced as in "on"

**Meaning**: The name *adho mukh shwān āsan* is made of four Sanskrit words: अधो *adho* means down, मुख *mukh* means face, श्वान *shwān* means dog and आसन *āsan* means pose.

**Benefits**: This invigorating pose increases flexibility while strengthening the children's arms and legs. It is said to be a rejuvenating stretch.

**How to do it**: Have the children start out on their hands and knees in a table-top position.

With their hands on the floor, ask them to lift their bottom towards the ceiling and straighten their legs as much as they can. They will look like an upside-down "V."

They can relax their head as they look down and try to keep their feet flat on the floor as they stretch.

If they can observe their breath while in the pose, that would be wonderful!

Then they can slowly return to the starting position.

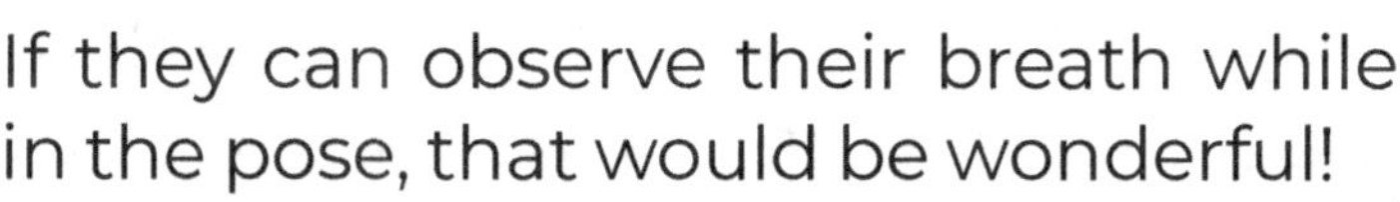

# Cat Poses
## मार्जरीआसन/बिडालासन Mārjārīāsan/Bidālāsan

**Pronunciation**: *mārjārīāsan/bidālāsan*, the *ā* is pronounced as in "on," the *ī* is pronounced as in "tea," the *a* is pronounced as in "hum,"the *i* is pronounced as "chin"

**Meaning**: In Sanskrit मार्जरी *mārjārī* means female cat and आसन *āsan* means pose. The word बिडाल *bidāl* means male cat and आसन *āsan* means pose.

**Benefits**: These poses relax the back and shoulders while stretching the neck and strengthening the arms and knees. They reduce stress, enhance focus and rejuvenate the body and mind.

These gentle poses are often performed one after the other creating a lovely flowing cat-like movement.

**How to do it**:

## Female Cat Pose मार्जरीआसन Mārjārīāsan

The children will start on their hands and knees in a table-top position.

Pay attention that their shoulders are over their hands, and their hips are over their knees. Their head and neck should be neutral, as the children attend their breath.

Ask them to breathe out as they slowly round their spine upwards. Their head will gently drop as they stretch their back, keeping their arms and legs in place.

They can hold the pose for a breath or two before beginning the second part.

## Male Cat Pose बिडालासन **Bidālāsan**

The children can breathe in while they slowly look up and arch their back inward.

They can hold the pose for a breath or two and then gently let their back and head return to the original position, while attending their breath.

The children can repeat the two poses, one after the other, several times.

## Bow Pose धनुरासन **Dhanurāsan**

**Pronunciation**: *dhanurāsan*, the *a* is pronounced as in "hum," the *u* is pronounced as in "full," the *ā* is pronounced as in "on"

**Meaning**: In Sanskrit धनुर *dhanur* means bow and आसन *āsan* means pose.

**Benefits**: This pose strengthens the back and leg muscles and helps improve posture. It also aids digestion.

**How to do it**: Have the children lie on their tummy, face down, with their hands by their sides.

They can breathe in as they bend their knees and grasp their ankles with their hands.

Their back will arch as their chest and thighs lift off the floor. Their body will resemble the shape of a bow.

If they can remember to watch their breath, that would be great!

# Boat Poses नावासन Nāvāsan

**Pronunciation**: *nāvāsan–ardh, paripurn*, the *ā* is pronounced as in "on," the *a* is pronounced as in "hum," the *i* is pronounced as in "chin," the *u* is pronounced as in "full

**Meaning**: In Sanskrit, नाव *nāv* means boat and आसन *āsan* means pose. अर्ध *ardh* means half and परिपूर्ण *paripurn* means full.

**Benefits**: These poses help build concentration and stamina while strengthening the abdomen and spine.

*Nāvāsan* can be completed in two parts. The children can start with *ardha nāvāsan*, half boat pose, and complete the pose with *paripurn nāvāsan*, the full boat pose.

**How to do it**:

## Half Boat Pose अर्ध नावासन Ardh Nāvāsan

Have the children sit on the floor with their knees bent and feet flat on the floor, hands resting slightly behind their hips, palms down.

Ask the children to lean back slightly, keeping their back straight, and lift their feet. They can try to make their shins parallel to the floor.

Then ask them to extend their arms forward, in line with their shoulders, and their palms facing each other.

## Full Boat Pose परिपूर्ण नावासन **Paripurn Nāvāsan**

When they feel comfortable, ask them to straighten their knees, keeping both legs together as one.

Their body will have the shape of the letter V, or a boat floating on the water, as the children balance on their bottom.

If they can remember to watch their breath, that would be wonderful!

## Lion Pose सिंघासन **Singhāsan**

**Pronunciation**: *singhāsan*, the *i* is pronounced as in "chin," the *ā* is pronounced as in "on," the *a* is pronounced as in "hum"

**Meaning**: In Sanskrit सिंघ *singh* means lion and आसन *āsan* is pose.

**Benefits**: This pose stimulates the platysma muscle, relieves tension in the face, throat and respiratory tract. It also calms the mind as it reduces stress and anger.

**How to do it**: Have the children sit tall on their heels with knees apart, arch their back slightly and breathe in.

Ask them to place the palms of their hands on their knees and spread out their fingers.

Then they can open their mouth, stick out their tongue, and breathe out a **ROAR** with strength and intent.

# Bridge Pose
## सेतुबन्धसर्वाङ्गासन Setu Bandh Sarvāngāsan

**Pronunciation**: *setu bandh sarvāngāsan*, the *e* is pronounced as "hay," the *u* is pronounced as "full," the *a* is pronounced as in "hum," the *ā* is pronounced as in "on"

**Meaning**: In Sanskrit सेतु *setu* means bridge, बन्ध *bandh* means build or lock, सर्व *sarv* means all, अङ्ग *ang* means limb and आसन *āsan* means  pose.

**Benefits**: This pose stretches and strengthens the back, shoulders, hips and legs. It is a restorative pose that also calms the mind and aids digestion.

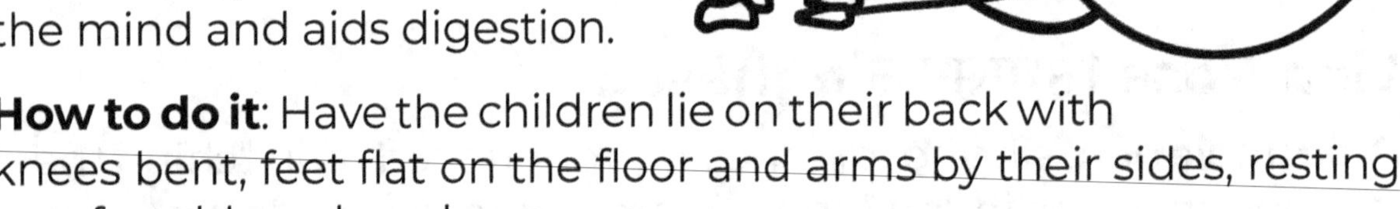

**How to do it**: Have the children lie on their back with knees bent, feet flat on the floor and arms by their sides, resting comfortably, palms down.

Ask them to gently lift their hips as high as they can, while keeping their arms on the floor. Make sure the children do not overstretch their back.

They can hold the pose for a comfortable time and watch their breath.

To finish the pose have them gently lower their hips to the floor.

# Gracious Pose भद्रासन Bhadrāsan

**Pronunciation**: *bhadrāsan*, the *a* is pronounced as in "hum," the *ā* is pronounced as in "on"

**Meaning**: The word भद्र *bhadra* in Sanskrit means auspicious, noble, gracious and gentle, while आसन *āsan* means pose.

**Benefits**: This pose helps to stretch the legs, inner thighs and hip area. It also calms the mind and grounds the body. This pose is great for meditation as it is comfortable and can be held easily.

**How to do it**: Have the children sit on the floor with their legs stretched in front of them.

Ask them to bend their knees and bring the soles of their feet together.

With their hands, have the children grasp their feet and pull them towards themselves, as far as is comfortable.

Remind the children to keep their back straight and allow their knees to relax gently towards the floor.

They can watch the rhythm of their own breath as they sit quietly holding the pose.

# Sphinx Pose सलम्ब भुजङ्गासन Salamb Bhujangāsan

**Pronunciation**: *salamb bhujangāsan*, the *a* is pronounced as in "hum," the *u* is pronounced as in "full," the *ā* is pronounced as in "on"

**Meaning**: In Sanskrit सलम्ब *salamb* means supported, भुजङ्ग *bhujang* means cobra and आसन *āsan* means pose. When held it looks like the sphinx.

**Benefits**: This pose stretches and strengthens the spine, shoulders, tummy and chest area, while rejuvenating the back. It also helps improve blood circulation thus relieving stress in the body.

**How to do it**: Have the children lie on their tummy, legs hip-width apart, chin on the floor and their hands under their shoulders.

Ask the children to breathe in as they slowly lift their head and chest off the floor.

At the same time, ask them to slide their hands forward and rest on their elbows and forearms. Their elbows should be below their shoulders.

They can hold this pose for few seconds or as long as they are comfortable and watch their breath.

When they are ready, they can gently breathe out as they lower their head and chest and rest their arms by their sides.

# Cobra Pose भुजङ्गासन **Bhujangāsan**

**Pronunciation**: *bhujangāsan*, the *u* is pronounced as in "full," the *a* is pronounced as in "hum," the *ā* is pronounced as in "on"

**Meaning**: भुजङ्ग *bhujang* means cobra in Sanskrit and आसन *āsan* means pose.

**Benefits**: This pose is great for increasing flexibility and strengthening the back, chest, arms and shoulders.

**How to do it**: Ask the children to lie on their tummy with legs hip-width apart.

With their forehead on the floor, ask them to place their hands under their shoulders, fingers pointing forward.

They can press their hips into the floor as they breathe in and gently lift their head, shoulders and upper chest while pressing on their palms and using the back muscles to lift them. They don't have to lift the upper body very high.

They can hold the pose for one or two breaths, then slowly breathe out as they relax and gently lower their body.

# Child Pose बालासन **Bālāsan**

**Pronunciation**: *bālāsan*, the *ā* is pronounced as in "on," the *a* is pronounced as in "hum"

**Meaning**: The word बाल *bāl* means child in Sanskrit and आसन *āsan* means pose.

**Benefits**: This restful pose is great for relaxing the back, neck and arms. It calms the body and mind as it releases tension and stress.

**How to do it**: Have the children start out on their hands and knees.

Ask them sit back on their heels and gently rest their chest on their thighs, as they breathe out. Their arms will be stretched forward as their palms and forehead rest on the floor.

Slowly they can bring their arms to rest alongside their body, palms upward.

They can stay in this resting pose and watch their breath. They can remain for a few breaths or for as long as they are comfortable.

# Corpse Pose or Immortal Pose शवासन **Shavāsan**

**Pronunciation**: *shavāsan*, the *a* is pronounced as in "hum," the *ā* is pronounced as in "on"

**Meaning**: The Sanskrit meaning of शव *shav* is corpse. The association of the corpse with death is transformed into immortality when the attention is placed on the Knower. आसन *āsan* means pose.

**Benefits**: This pose helps rejuvenate the child mentally and physically. It is a pose of total relaxation.

**How to do it**: Have the children lie on their back and close their eyes.

Ask them to rest their arms comfortably by their sides, palms upwards. Their legs should be comfortable and relaxed.

They can take a few deep breaths to relax their body into the pose    and hold for some time.

To come out of the pose the children should roll over slowly onto their side. With bended knees, they can use their arms to push themselves up.

# Warrior Poses वीरभद्रासन Vīrabhadrāsan

**Pronunciation**: *vīrabhadrāsan*, the *ī* is pronounced as in "tea," the *a* is pronounced as in "hum," the *ā* is pronounced as in "on"

**Meaning**: In Sanskrit वीर *vīr* means hero, भद्र *bhadra* means friend and आसन *āsan* means pose.

There are three poses called *virabhadrāsan*, named for the warrior Virabhadra from Hindu mythology. The essence of the story of Virabhadra is that Lord Shiv married Sati, the daughter of King Daksha. According to legend, King Daksha disapproved of their union and cut his daughter off from the family. There are different versions of this story, however, in every version Sati eventually kills herself. In his grief, Lord Shiv creates the great warrior Virabhadra to exact his revenge.

**Benefits**: These poses are excellent for balance, coordination, flexibility, focus, concentration, power, strength and confidence.

**A hint for keeping balance**: Ask the children to pick a point in front of them to stare at. Focusing on one point will help them with their balance.

**How to do it**:

## Warrior Pose 1 वीरभद्रासन १ Vīrabhadrāsan 1

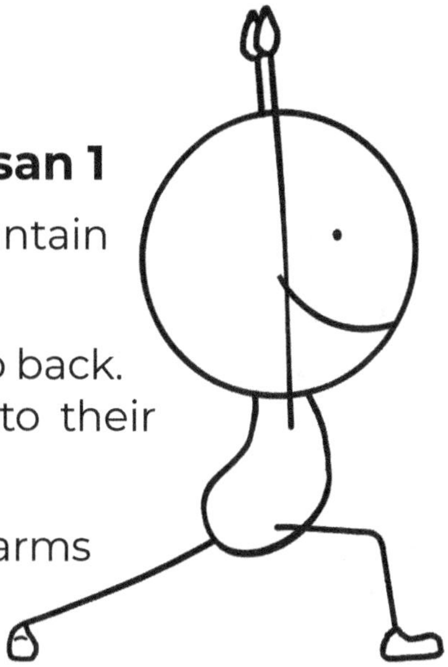

Have the children stand tall as in the mountain pose.

Ask them to breathe out and take a big step back. Their back foot should be perpendicular to their forward foot.

Have them breathe in as they raise their arms above their head and place their palms together.

Then ask them to bend their forward knee so that it is directly over their ankle as they stretch their back leg, keeping it straight.

They can hold the pose for a few breaths.

## Warrior Pose 2 वीरभद्रासन २ Vīrabhadrāsan 2

Have the children stand tall as in the mountain pose.

Ask them to breathe out and take a big step back. Their back foot should be perpendicular to their forward foot.

Have them breathe in as they extend their arms sideways at shoulder height.

Then ask them to bend their forward knee so that it is directly over their ankle as they stretch their back leg, keeping it straight.

They can hold the pose for a few breaths.

## Warrior Pose 3 वीरभद्रासन ३ Vīrabhadrāsan 3

Have the children stand tall as in the mountain pose.

Ask them to shift their weight to stand on one leg.

Have the children breathe in as they extend their arms forward at shoulder height.

Then ask them to lift their back leg off the ground, so that their arms, torso and lifted leg are parallel with the floor.

**Hints for the Warrior Poses**:
- The children should repeat each of the poses with the other foot forward.
- You can have them perform each warrior pose in a series.
- These poses are fun to do with partners, in groups or in rows.

# Sun Salutation Poses
## सूर्यनमस्कारासन Sūrya Namaskārāsan

**Pronunciation**: *sūrya namaskārāsan*, the *ū* is pronounced as in "hoop," the *a* is pronounced as in "hum," the *ā* is pronounced as in "on"

**Meaning**: In Sanskrit the word सूर्य *surya* means the sun, नमस् *namas* means to bow in respect, कार *kār* is the performance of action and आसन *āsan* means pose.

**Benefits**: The Sun Salutation is a series of poses that creates a lovely fluid movement, as one pose flows into the next.

It can be fun to teach the individual poses separately and then practice some poses together to focus on the flow of one pose into the next. You can then group a number of poses together until the children are able to complete all the poses of the Sun Salutation. It's like a beautiful dance.

You can also pair or cluster different poses to create your own unique salutation.

**How to do it**:

### Step 1: Mountain Pose ताडासन Tādāsan

Have the children stand tall, both feet facing forward, hip-width apart, arms by their sides. Ask the children to breathe in as they gently bend their elbows and press their palms together towards their chest and breathe out.

### Step 2: Raised Hands Pose
### ऊर्ध्व हास्तासन Ūrdhva Hāstāsan

Have the children breathe in as they slowly raise their arms above their head slightly tilting backward.

### Step 3: Forward-Fold Pose उत्तानासन Uttānāsan

Ask the children breathe out as they bend forward to place the palms of their hands on the floor; they can bend their knees if they need to.

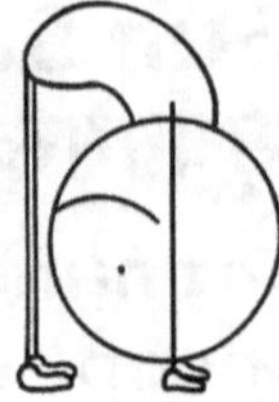

### Step 4: Equestrian Pose
### अश्व सञ्चलनासन Ashwa Sanchalanāsan

With their hands on the floor, have the children breathe in and extend one foot back while the forward foot remains between their hands.

### Step 5: Downward-Facing Dog Pose
### अधोमुखश्वानासन Adho Mukh Shwānāsan

Ask the children to breathe out as they bring their forward foot alongside their back foot, creating an upside-down V shape with straight arms and legs. Their head and neck should be relaxed.

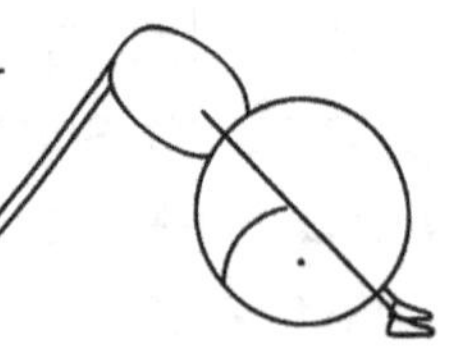

### Step 6: Cobra Pose भुजङ्गासन Bhujangāsan

**Part 1:** Ask the children to breathe in as they lower their body to the floor so they are lying on their tummy.

**They will now do the poses in reverse order**

### Step 7: Cobra Pose भुजङ्गासन Bhujangāsan

**Part 2:** With their hands under their shoulders, ask the children to breathe in and gently lift their head, shoulders and upper chest.

### Step 8: Downward-Facing Dog Pose
### अधोमुखश्वानासन Adho Mukh Shwānāsan

Ask the children to breathe out as they slowly raise their hips and come back to the upside-down V shape with straight arms and legs.

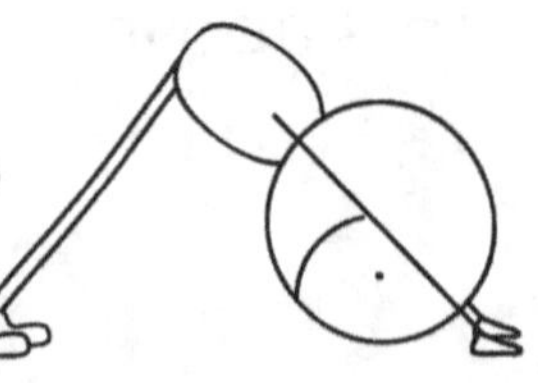

## Step 9: Equestrian Pose
## अश्व सञ्चलनासन Ashwa Sanchalanāsan

They can breathe in as they move their foot forward (the same foot they moved forward earlier) placing it between their hands, then they can arch their back and tilt their head upwards.

## Step 10: Forward-Fold Pose उत्तानासन Uttānāsan

Ask the children to breathe out as they slowly rise up bringing their back foot forward to meet their other foot, placing their palms on the floor.

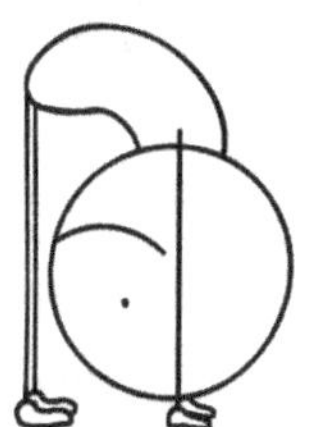

## Step 11: Raised Hands Pose
## ऊर्ध्व हास्तासन Ūrdhva Hāstāsan

The children can breathe in as they slowly raise their arms above their head slightly tilting backward.

## Step 12: Mountain Pose ताडासन Tādāsan

Have the children breathe out, stand tall with both feet facing forward, hip-width apart, while they gently bend their elbows and press their palms together towards their chest and salute the sun.

You can have the children repeat the Sun Salutation Poses by moving the other foot first.

# Chapter 5

# The Play of Action, Karma Yoga

Within the heart of every man is the desire to improve, to become greater than he is, whatever his understanding of this greatness may be. (Swami Shyam, 1983, *Why Meditation*, p 2,

The meaning of Karma Yoga is action united with intelligence. This chapter, The Play of Action, Karma Yoga, is comprised of selected activities, games and skills to complement and enrich the topics and themes of the *Timeless Tales*. The activities can be conducted individually or in group.

As children develop, their attention becomes riveted on whatever they find an attraction to. Most often they are attracted to objects, people, toys, games and activities that move with kinetic energy. This movement matches the energy of the mind, which is always moving and changing. It is therefore important to present the mind with objects and activities that attract, charm and guide the children towards their own goodness and well-being.

I remember my teacher, Swami Shyam, being asked what he thought about spoiling children. He responded in the most delightfully playful way, saying, "You must spoil the children into goodness."

This collection of learning-centred skills and activities seeks to enrich and excite an openness in children towards goodness, meditation, learning and having fun with friends. The activities were selected for their specific skill sets, in different areas of development, such as self-concept, communication skills, linear thinking, cooperation, focusing and examining, reading, language and sensory perception as well as providing a healthy respect for human dignity.

Movement and stillness are essential ingredients for children to develop in a healthy and balanced way. These skills and activities, along with meditation and guidance, help the children observe and critique their own actions and reactions in a safe environment—such as how they feel when a particular person talks to them, interacts with them or even enters a room.

Through observing everyday occurrences, the children's sense of judgement becomes refined, their confidence gets built and they develop a greater understanding of their own mechanism.

Through games and activities, the children become more adept at pinpointing their own actions and reactions to ideas and situations. Observation of their own actions and reactions helps them recognize situations, behaviours and people they would like to embrace, change, alter or avoid. This gives them skills of choice—to choose to move in a direction that will provide them with their own sense of ease and well-being.

Through continued observation, the children may witness interactions where friends do not agree with them or with other friends' thoughts and ideas. Through activities, interactions and meditation on the Knower, they will come to know where agreement lies. Agreement lies where people are united. People are eternally united in their source, which is the Knower.

> Therefore, the secret of successful thinking is to become
> united with your own true nature first—then simply enjoy.
> (Swami Shyam, 1994, *Vision of Oneness*, p 61)

The target of the Knower Curriculum is to provide children with the knowledge, skills and opportunity to come to know their own true nature, which is intelligence, joy, delight and freedom.

Enjoy!

# Activities and Games

## Back-to-Back Communication

This activity is a fun way to highlight verbal communication skills.

One child is the direction-giver while the other is the receiver. The direction-giver must articulate his or her directions to his or her partner, the receiver. The receiver must listen carefully and ask for clarification when needed.

It is fun when this activity has a time limit. (2-4 minutes)

**Materials:**
- two large identical pieces of paper, one for each child (younger children may need the paper to have left and right indicators)
- two identical sets of coloured shapes, one set for each child

**Procedure:**
Children play in pairs.

Instruct the children to sit back-to-back with their partner. Each child should have a large piece of paper and a set of coloured shapes that are identical to those of his or her partner.

Each child should not be able to see his or her partner's paper or shapes.

The child who is the direction-giver will make a design on the piece of paper, using the shapes. Once the design is complete, the direction-giver will verbally instruct the receiver how to recreate the design on his or her piece of paper using the identical shapes.

If the child receiving instructions has difficulty understanding something, he or she may verbally ask for clarification. Neither child may turn around to look at his or her partner's design until the task is completed.

Upon completion the children will look at both designs to see if they are identical. The partners can gauge how successful their verbal communication skills were, both in giving directions and receiving them. You can ask the children to reverse roles.

**Variations:**
Sitting back-to-back, the children can be given identical pages from a colouring book. The direction-giver would colour in the page and then give instructions to the receiver to produce an identical picture.

*Please feel free to modify this activity to suit your children's ages, needs and abilities.

**Follow-up:**
Observations can be shared and discussed with the class. You can ask such question as:

- What challenges did you face when giving directions and receiving them?
- How did you feel when the other person did not understand your directions?
- How did you feel when you did not understand the directions you were given?
- Did you find the activity difficult?
- Which did you prefer, being the direction-giver or the receiver?

# Balance Scales

Learning to make balance scales can be fun. The children can learn to balance many different kinds of objects.

**Materials:**
- a hanger
- a ball of string or yarn
- scissors and hole punch
- two identical receptacles, such as paper cups, vegetable containers, picnic bowls or small beach pails
- a ruler or tape measure
- masking or packing tape

**Procedure:**
Measure two pieces of string 30-60 cm (1-2 ft) each, and cut. Check to make sure both strings are even in length.

Make a hole on opposite sides of each receptacle. The holes will be used for attaching the string. If you are using identical beach pails with handles, you can skip this step.

Tie the string to each side of the cup. If you are using a beach pail, place the string around the handle and make a knot at the end.

Tape the string with the receptacle hanging from it on one side of the hanger. Repeat on the other side, making sure the strings are the same length.

The children can have fun comparing the weights of different toys, coins, pencils, erasers or blocks—any item that can fit in the receptacle can be weighed and compared with another.

**Alternative:**
You can present the children with standard weight measures, such as coins or paper clips. Ask the children to find out how many coins are equal to a pencil or toy.

# Blindfold Games

Children will learn about the value of the sense of sight and the value of the other senses. These activities are great for developing communication skills, heightening awareness of the other senses and active listening.

## What Is It?
**Materials:**
- blindfolds
- box of toys—stuffed toys, action figures, etc.

**Procedure:**
Have the children work in pairs. One child will put on a blindfold while the other selects an object from the box of toys.

The blindfolded child will use his or her hands to examine the object, describe what he or she is feeling and then guess what it is. Then the children can switch roles.

## Open Locks Blindfolded
**Materials:**
- blindfolds
- a padlock with a key

**Procedure:**
Give the child a padlock and key. Blindfold the child and ask him or her to try to unlock the padlock.

## Drawing and Writing Blindfolded
**Materials:**
- blindfolds
- paper and pencil, or white board and markers

**Procedure:**
With a piece of paper or white board, have the blindfolded children try to write their names or draw smiley faces.

# Blowing Bubbles

This is a an excellent way to explore what happens when a child breathes differently.

**Materials:**
- paper cups
- water
- straws

**Procedure:**
Give each child a paper cup half-filled with water, and a straw. Let them inhale gently through their nose, place the straw in their mouth and blow out through the straw into the cup of water.

The children can observe how the air streams out of the straw and creates bubbles in the water. You can have them try different types of breath to observe the difference in the types of bubbles they create. For instance, they can discover the difference between bubbles created with a long, slow exhalation and bubbles made with short, sharp bursts of air.

**Alternative:**
Another way is to blow bubbles through a bubble wand using liquid soap. Children can observe what kind of breath creates the best bubbles—long slow and steady or short and powerful.

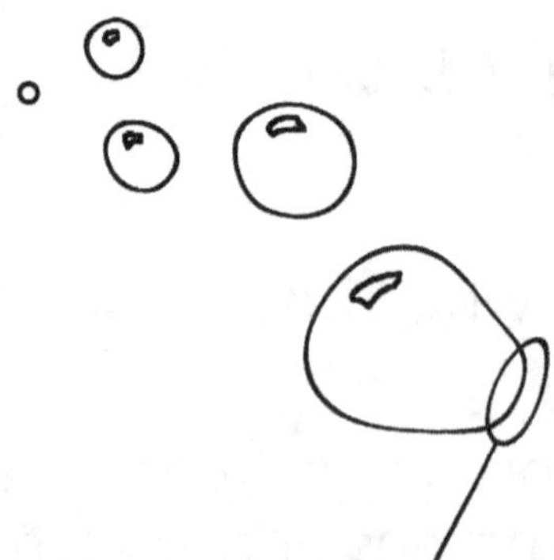

# Broken Telephone

Any time a message is passed along by a number of people, the information can become distorted in the process. This activity demonstrates that you can't always trust what you hear. This game is popular among children everywhere.

**Procedure:**

The children can either sit or stand in a circle or in a straight line.

The teacher can give a piece of paper with a word or phrase written on it to the first child.

The first child will whisper those words into the ear of the child next to him or her. Remind the children to use their hands to cover the ear of their listener.

The child who heard the words will then cover the ear of the next child, and whisper what he or she has heard.

This will be repeated until the last child has heard the words.

The last child will say out loud what he or she heard. Then each child, going in opposite order—from last to first—will say out loud what he or she heard.

The first child can reveal the piece of paper with the original message.

**Discussion:**

This activity is a metaphor for cumulative errors. It demonstrates the unreliability of the mind's recollection, and the inaccuracies that can result.

Errors accumulate in the retelling. The words spoken by the last player may differ significantly from those spoken by the first, usually with humorous results.

# Building Bridges

This group activity focuses on problem-solving and cooperation skills.

**Materials:**
- old newspapers and masking tape

**Procedure:**
The children are placed in groups of six or eight children.

The object of this activity is to build a bridge out of newspapers and masking tape (or sticks and string, or any materials of your choosing)

Select a test object with particular height and weight specifications, such as a box that is about 30–60 cm (1-2 ft) in height and width, and 1–2 kg (2-3 lb) in weight.

The group is asked to build a structure that is high enough for the box to slide under and strong enough to support its weight.

The children are asked to complete the bridge in two stages:

1. The Planning Stage: During this stage the children can measure the box, feel its weight, and make plans with their group about how to construct a structure to meet the requirements. The children are given about 10 minutes.
2. The Building Stage: During the next 15 minutes, the group will build their structure according to their plans. During this time they cannot touch the test object, the box.

At the end of the building stage, their structure is tested for height, to see if the box is able to slide under the bridge, and for strength, to see if the bridge can hold the weight of the box.

After the bridge has been tested—it is evident whether the structure passed the test or not—the children can share and discuss the group processes they experienced.

The teacher can ask questions such as:
- How were decisions made in your group?
- Was a leader chosen, if so how did this happen?
- How were arguments settled?
- How were responsibilities divided amongst the people in the group?

The cooperative group process can be very illuminating.

## Alternatives:
Ship building. Have the children build a floating device that will float and hold a certain weight.

Elevator

Pulley system

# Coat of Arms

Throughout history the coat of arms has been used as a symbol of identity for a family, kingdom or country. It is a design in the form of a shield or shield-shaped pattern.

The children can design their own personal coat of arms or one for a character in a timeless tale, to indicate their merits, achievements and abilities.

**Materials:**
- coat of arms outlines are provided
- markers, paints, crayons, magazines, glue and scissors

The personal coat of arms is divided into quadrants. You can have the children design each section in answer to the following suggestions. Some personal coats of arms can have a centre section for the child's picture.

Below the Coat of Arms is a place where the children can write a **motto** describing themselves.

1. A symbol of something that represents who you are
2. A symbol of something that represents your greatest achievement
3. A symbol of something you want to accomplish
4. A symbol of your favorite activity or possession
5. Centre: The children can draw themselves.

# Coat of Arms

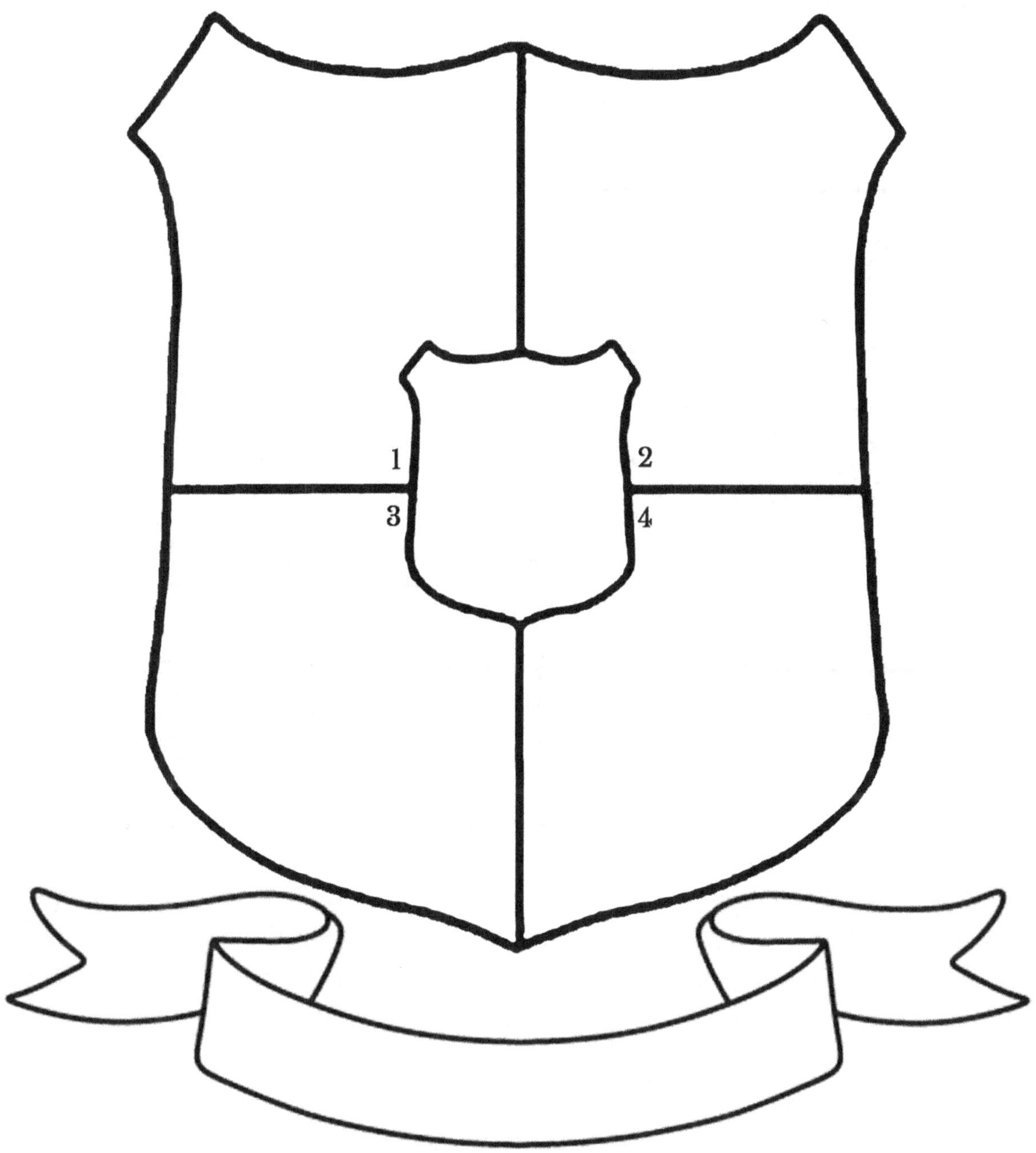

# Coat of Arms

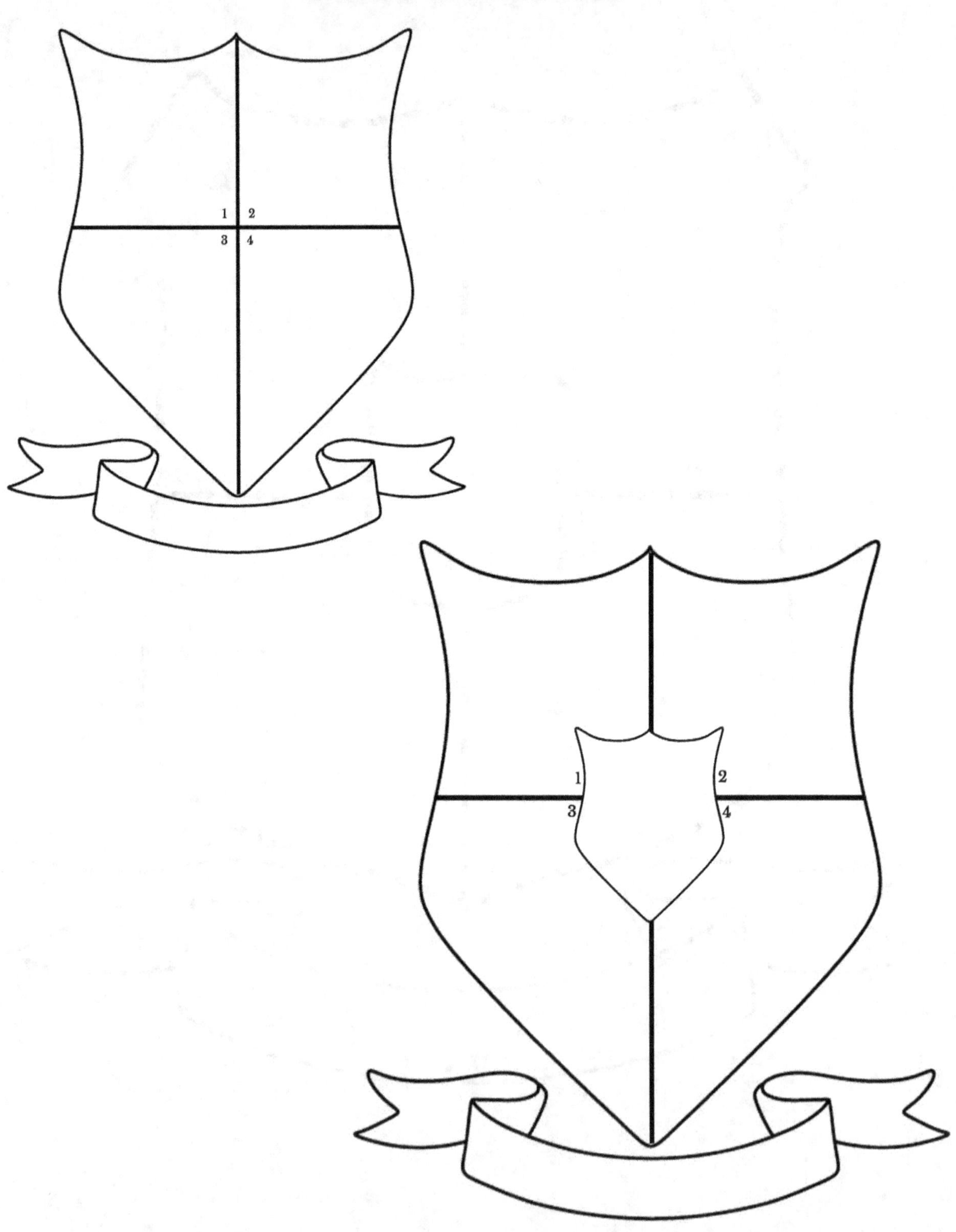

# Commercials

Children are familiar with commercials as methods of advertising products. Using themes from the timeless tales, children can create commercials to advertise abstract or unobvious perceptions as their products. Unobvious perceptions would include such products as happiness, freedom, peace of mind, a particular emotion or skill, to name a few.

The chosen medium will determine the materials. The children can advertise in a magazine or newspaper, a poster or billboard, a brochure, on radio, television, an app or an online commercial.

**Procedure:**
The children can choose which abstract perception they would like to make their commercial about. They might like to advertise a unique outlook, habit or skill. They can try to figure out how to advertise such things as developing confidence, how to remain easy or what habit someone might like to have or not have. You can suggest that the commercials be humorous and thoughtful.

The children work alone or in groups and can select the medium of their commercial (print, audio or video) and the product they would like to advertise.

They can share their skills with each other, such as art, photography, music, video, narration, script writing, etc. They can even advertise their skills so others may like to engage them.

Creating commercials of abstract perceptions is a fun way for children to stretch their thinking as they explore deeper aspects.

I always enjoyed the commercials my students prepared.

# Plan Your Commercial

Name_______________________________________________

Timeless Tale _______________________________________

Date________________________________________________


What is your product? ___________________________
(abstract perception)

___________________________________________________

___________________________________________________

What medium will you use for your commercial?
(print, billboard, radio, television, online, video)

___________________________________________________

___________________________________________________

Who is your target audience?____________________
(what type of person)

___________________________________________________

Where can your product be obtained?______________

___________________________________________________

Why will people want your product? ______________

___________________________________________________

Why is your product better than others?___________

___________________________________________________

When will your product be available?______________

___________________________________________________

# Compass and Mapmaking Skills

A compass is a device that detects the Earth's magnetic field. Global Positioning Systems (GPS) are the most advanced way to determine your position on Earth and the direction you would like to go. GPS utilizes satellites in orbit around the Earth, but before GPS, the way to know which way you were sailing when at sea was to use constellations or a compass.

Teaching compass and mapmaking skills to children is a great way to cultivate abstract thinking and problem solving.

## How to make a Compass

**Materials:**
- bowl of water
- sewing needle or pin
- magnet
- cork, or small piece of craft foam or piece of paper

**Procedure:**
Cut a small circle from a material that will float in water (cork, piece of foam or paper)

The next step is to turn the sewing needle or pin into a magnet. To do this, stroke the needle across the magnet thirty to forty times in **one direction only**, not back and forth. The needle will now be magnetized.

Next, place the needle on the circle of floating material (cork, foam or paper) and place it in the water. Try to place it in the centre of the bowl, keeping it away from the edges. The needle will slowly begin to revolve and eventually the needle will point north and south.

You can check the accuracy using a real compass or an app.

With a marker, nail polish or paint, colour the tip that is facing north to distinguish it from south.

## How magnets work

Every magnet has a north and south pole. A compass is a small magnet that aligns itself with the north and south poles of the Earth's magnetic field. As the needle is stroked across the magnet, in one direction, it becomes magnetized and aligned with the magnet. The magnetized needle then aligns itself with the Earth's magnetic field when it is placed on the surface of the water.

## Compass Activities

There are many compass games and direction games that you can play with children of all ages and abilities. Even simple games such as "**Simon Says**..." can be fun as you send the children en-route to different places in the classroom.

## A Compass Game

Make a map of the classroom using direction skills, indicating how many paces north, south, etc. to reach the windows, the cloakroom, the cupboard, the blackboard, etc.

This game can be tailored to the children's ages or level of compass familiarity. For this game you'll need a compass, a marker and a direction sheet.

This problem-solving game can be played either in teams or individually.

When creating the direction sheets, the key is to make sure they will lead their teams back to the starting point. This is how you'll know whether they followed the directions correctly.

A simple direction sheet might look something like this:

1. Take 5 steps south
2. Take 10 steps east
3. Take 20 steps north
4. Take 15 steps west
5. Take 15 steps south
6. Take 5 steps east.

## Mapmaking and Map Planning

You can provide real maps or printouts of the whole world or particular geographic areas.

Using markers, have children chart their course from one place to another. They will have to decide whether they travel by land, sea or air.

You can ask the children to chart a course to a place they might like to visit.

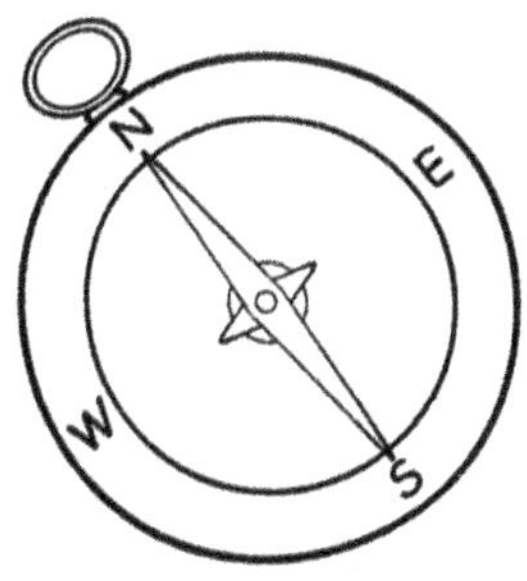

# Complaint Report

This activity gives children the opportunity to isolate events and bring into focus different points of view. In this way they are given the opportunity to see from the viewpoint of someone else.

**Materials:**
- complaint report
- pencils or pens

**Procedure:**
Ask the children to fill out the complaint report from the point of view of a character from one of the timeless tales.

For example: From the story "The Fox and the Camel," a complaint report could be filled out by the farmer, by Camel, or by Fox. In "Truth Story" complaint reports could be filled out by the hunter, each of the men meditating or even the deer.

# Complaint Report

Date ___________________________________________

Timeless Tale ____________________________________

Name of character filing complaint__________________

Contact information ______________________________

_______________________________________________

## Your Complaint

**When did it happen?**_______________________________

_______________________________________________

**Where did it happen?**______________________________

_______________________________________________

**What happened?** _________________________________

_______________________________________________

_______________________________________________

**How would you like this complaint resolved?**___________

_______________________________________________

_______________________________________________

## Doctor's Diagnosis

The children can interview each other, one as doctor and the other as patient, to diagnose abstract, unobvious perceptual ailments, such as uneasiness, fear of criticism or a bad habit.

The child playing the patient can fill out the patient registration form from the point of view of a character from one of the timeless tales, noting the character's symptoms.

The child playing the role of doctor can think of remedies for the patient's abstract symptoms. The patient (character) can try out the remedy to see if the suggestion works.

Patient Registration forms and Doctor's Diagnosis forms are provided.

# Doctor's Diagnosis

Date _______________________________________________

Timeless Tale _______________________________________

Name of Patient _____________________________________

| Consultation | Diagnosis |
|---|---|
| | |
| **Prescription** | **Cure** |

# Patient's Registration



Date_______________________________________________

Timeless Tale_______________________________________

_________________________________________________

Name of character____________________________________

_________________________________________________

Contact information___________________________________

_________________________________________________

## Your Symptoms

What are your symptoms?________________________________

_________________________________________________

When did they begin?__________________________________

_________________________________________________

How are you feeling?__________________________________

_________________________________________________

What happened?______________________________________

_________________________________________________

_________________________________________________

_________________________________________________

Additional information

_________________________________________________

_________________________________________________

# Family Tree

This activity will help children understand the meaning of lineage, ancestry and heritage.

A family tree is a diagram or visual representation generally showing the relationship between people of several generations.

You can make a family tree as complex or as simple as you like. It can represent centuries of generations or it can be the representation of a simple nuclear family.

Understanding genealogy can help children understand the relationships between relatives. When I was reading the "Harry Potter" series and watching "Game of Thrones," I remember looking up the family trees in order to have a fuller understanding of the relationships of some of the characters to each other.

You can have the children make a family tree of the relationships of story characters from a timeless tale.

The family tree activity can be as personal or impersonal as you like.

Provided are some family tree ideas. You can also have the children make their own designs.

# Family Tree

Grandfather
Grandmother
Father
Mother
Uncle
Aunt
Brother
Sister
Me
Cousin
Cousin

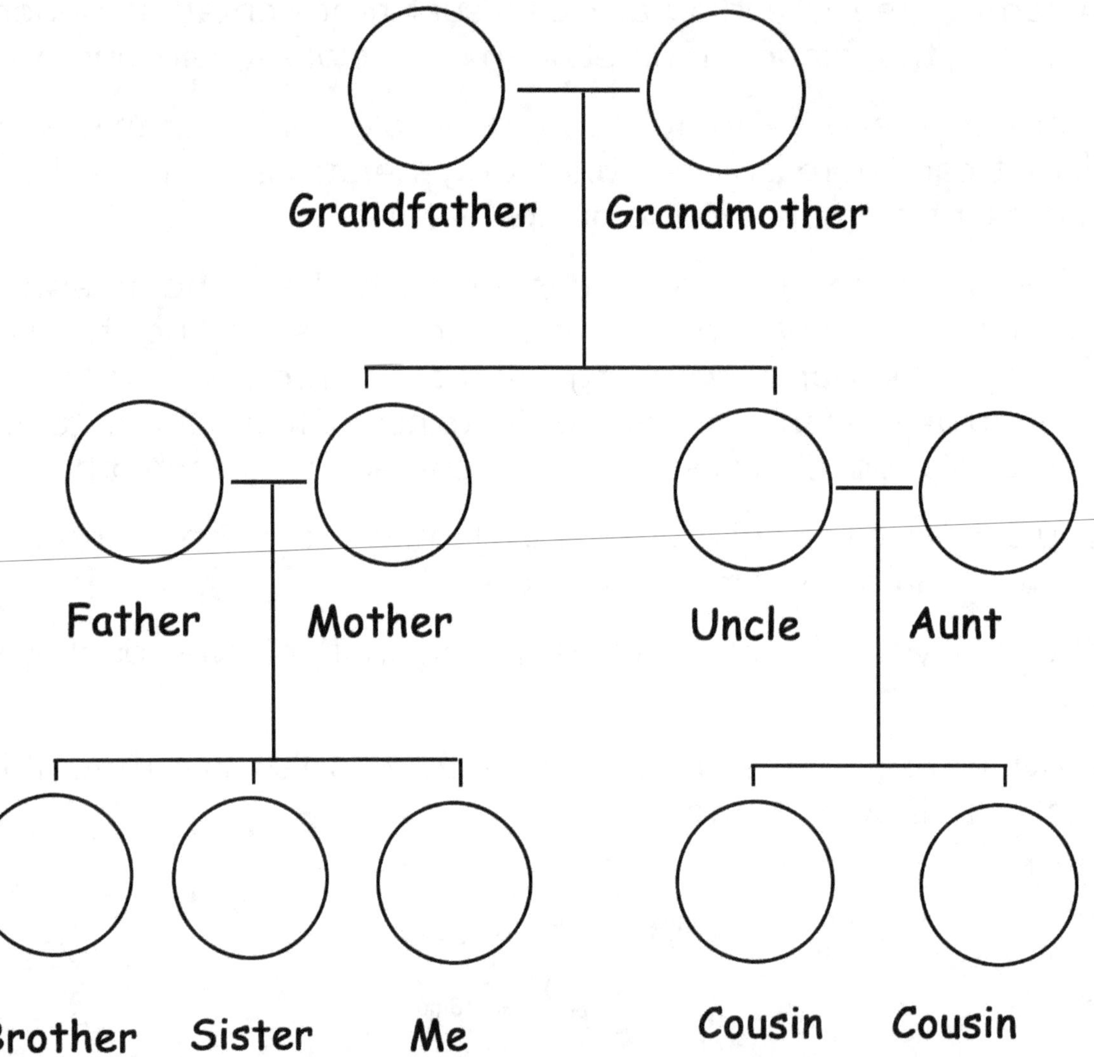

# Fingerprints

Everyone is unique and different. One of the unique differences are people's fingerprints.

**Materials:**
- ink pads
- paper

**Procedure:**
Have the children use the ink pads to ink up their thumbs and fingers. (If you have a fingerprint scanner or fingerprint app, you can have fun with that as well.)

Have each child make a profile of their fingerprints.

The class can discuss the uniqueness of each person's prints and how they are used in so many ways, from turning on a cell phone to identifying criminals.

A fun activity with fingerprints, is to have the children decorate their fingerprints, using coloured markers, to create fingerprint people or fingerprint animals.

Each creation will be unique to the child's own fingerprint.

# Grumpy T-Shirt

Design your own Grumpy T-Shirt.

Using the paper T-shirt provided, have the children draw their thoughts, feelings and emotions in the designated areas.

1. Draw a grumpy picture in the circle.
2. Write a grumpy sentence on the front pocket.
3. Write a grumpy number on the patch on the sleeve.
4. Choose two grumpy colours for the stripes on the sleeve.

You can also have the children design their own Grumpy T-Shirt. However, if you are feeling adventurous you can have them draw on real T-shirts.

# Grumpy T-Shirt

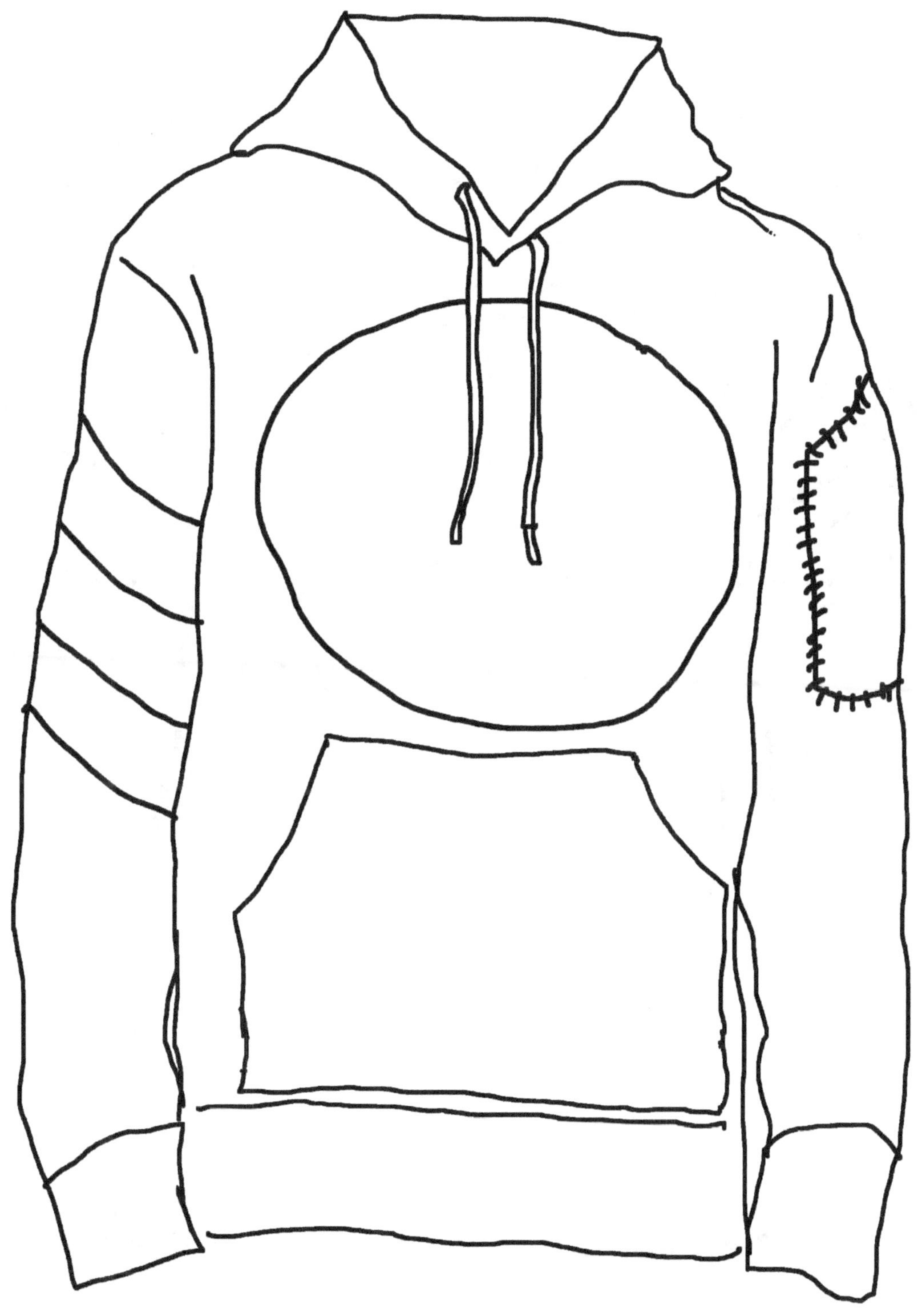

# Grumpy T-Shirt

# Mala

A mala is a string of beads that is used in meditation in order to count mantras or breaths. The word "mala" means a garland in Sanskrit. A mala is commonly referred to as a string of prayer beads.

Mantra meditation using a mala is a tactile way for a child to focus his or her mind and energy during meditation. The child's power of concentration is developed through the recitation of a mantra.

A full mala is 108 beads plus one extra bead called the Guru bead, which is typically different from the counting beads. The Guru bead is where the child begins and ends a round of counting mantras or breaths. The Guru bead is a marker for the child's fingers so that he or she will know when one round is complete.

The word *Guru* is comprised of two words, *gu*, meaning darkness or ignorance; and *ru* meaning remover. The meaning of the word Guru refers to the one who removes darkness or ignorance. The word Guru also connotes a teacher as one who reveals or imparts the knowledge of enlightenment, the knowledge of the Self or Knower.

A hand mala is smaller in the number of beads than a full mala (108 beads plus the Guru bead) Traditionally, a hand mala is a quarter the number of beads—27 beads plus the Guru bead.

When using a mala with children, depending on their age, they might find using the hand mala more manageable. Of course any string of beads with any number can be used. But it is recommended that there be a Guru bead in order to keep count of the rounds.

**Technique:**
Have the children hold the mala in one hand. They will start the round from the Guru bead. With the beads resting between their thumb and middle, or ring, finger, they will begin their round of

pulling the beads towards them. They can use either the index or middle finger to pull the beads. There are other styles of mala where the thumb is used to pull the beads. The children should feel comfortable with whatever style they choose.

As each bead it held and thereby counted, the breath or mantra is repeated, until the Guru bead is reached again. Then one round is complete. The child can choose to do another round if he or she likes.

For example:

Repeat *Amaram Hum* on the first bead,
*Madhuram Hum* on the second,
*Amaram Hum* on the third,
and *Madhuram Hum* on the fourth,
until the round is complete.

Repeat *Om* on the first bead,
*Om* on the second,
*Om* on the third,
and *Om* on the fourth,
until the round is complete.

The children may just like to count the beads, 1, 2, 3, 4, 5, and so on... as their fingers circle the mala beads.

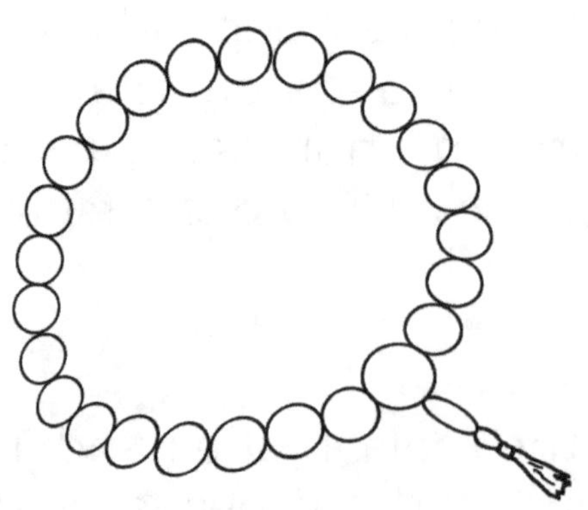

# Memory Games

These suggested activities can be adapted for all ages and for all stories.

## Memory Cards

Mix up a deck of cards or two suits from the deck.

Lay the cards out in rows, face down.

The children will take turns turning over the cards. The first child will turn over any two cards. If the two cards match, the child will keep them. If they don't match, the child will return the cards back to their places, face down.

Each child should try to remember what was on each remaining card and where it was located.

The game is over when all the cards have been matched.

The child with the most sets of cards, wins.

## Three Cups

Have one child line up three paper cups and place a small object under one of the cups.

The child can switch the cups back and forth into new positions while the other children watch closely to see if they can follow the movement of the object under the cup.

The children watching can take turns guessing which cup the object is hiding under.

The children can take turns hiding the object.

## Word Chain

Choose a topic, such as food or any topic from one of the Timeless Tales.

The first child says a word, the second one says that word plus adds his or her own word on the topic. The third child says the first two words in order, plus adds his or her own...and so forth.

Continue until someone breaks the word chain.

## Memory Match

This is fun to play in pairs.

You can have one child set up coins, or any type of play object, in a random pattern.

The other child is given ten seconds to stare at the objects trying to memorise the pattern.

Once memorised, ask the child to close his or her eyes and try to see the pattern in his or her mind.

The child who created the pattern can then remove, add or replace one item.

When the child with closed eyes opens them, she or he has to pinpoint what is different.

The children can take turns being the arranger and the memorizer.

# Mirror Breath

Mirror breath displays a visible representation of the child's own breath.

**Materials:**
- a mirror

**Procedure:**
Each child could have a personal mirror or they can share space on a larger mirror. If mirrors are unavailable you can have the children breathe onto a window glass.

Have each child first inhale and then slowly exhale through their mouth to create a fog on the mirror or glass.

You can have the children try different exhalation techniques to see if their breath looks different when they exhale differently. They can play around with their out breath to see if they make a better fog with a faster or slower breath.

They also can make little drawings on the fogged mirror with their fingers to indicate how they feel.

# Mirrors

*Mirrors don't talk, they only reflect.*

In this activity, the children can be placed in pairs or groups and each child should have a chance to be the leader. This is a silent game because "mirrors don't talk, they only reflect."

Give the children a set amount of time for each round, for example 60 seconds. During that time the leader can move slowly and deliberately while their friend(s) mirror the leader's movements, as if they were their mirror image.

The leader may make faces, wave their arms or legs, turn from side to side, stand on one foot—anything they can imagine, within reason.

It should be a silent activity. The leader should move slowly and smoothly so that their "mirror images" can follow along in sync. After 60 seconds, have the children switch roles.

## Variation:
The teacher can be the leader and the children can all be in the mirror.

This is a great way to teach and practice hatha yoga poses. The children in my classes always enjoyed this game and paid very special attention to the poses when they were in the mirror.

# My World

In this activity the children learn respect for personal space

**Materials:**
* a ball of string or yarn
* scissors

**Procedure:**
Measure and cut the string or yarn to the height of each child.

When each child and the teacher have their own measured string, tell the children that their string represents their world. Their world is as big as they are.

Ask each child to make a closed circle with their world. You can tell them that when they are in their world, they can do what they like. But they must stay within the boundaries of their string-world. In this way each child will make a closed circle on the floor, which indicates the boundaries of their string world.

You can tell the children that they can join their world with someone else's. Each child can place one end of their string on one end of another person's and make a larger closed circle using the strings of both.

The children will notice that when they join their world with another person's world, they have a larger space. They also come to learn that they must share it equally with the other person, because each has contributed to the space with their string.

You can have two pairs of children join together and so forth, until the entire class has joined their worlds to form one large world.

The experience of joining individual and group worlds into one world generates interesting topics for discussion. Some topics can be the need for consideration of others, the need for rules of conduct and the idea that each child in the string world has contributed their own space to the creation of that string world, and what that means.

*I can remember when I was a teacher and we played "My World," I discovered that the children kept their strings in their pockets. When they wanted to be alone, or sit privately with a friend, they would sit in their string world undisturbed. The other children actually respected their privacy.*

# Name Games

## What's In A Name

The purpose of this activity is for each child is to understand the meaning of their own name.

Historically, names were mostly descriptive words or phrases to help identify people and distinguish them from others. For example, Phillip means lover of horses, Peter means rock or stone, Margaret means pearl, Judith means admired or praised, Ann, derived from Hanna, means full of grace.

Using either baby name books or the internet, the children can begin to investigate and discover the meaning and origin of the name they were given.

### Discussion Topics:

What function do names serve? Names help us identify and talk about specific individuals. You might say that a person's name is like their personal brand, or part of their identity.

Who decides what name a person gets? Most often it is their parents. Different cultures have different ways of bestowing names on their young. Some children have nicknames. Ask the children if they know any other way of ascribing a name.

Some cultures ascribe names to children according to qualities they see or would like to see in the child. Other cultures pass along names to their children from either living or deceased relatives and some ascribe names according to their position in the family.

## Name Game

Have the children sit in a circle and say their name and one word that describes them; they can use gestures along with words. The next person will repeat the first name and word, and add their own name and word, this will continue around the circle until it reaches the first person, who has to try to repeat all the names and attributes of the children in the group.

## Describe Yourself

Children's names are important. It is one of the ways they identify themselves. They can use their name to tell more about themselves, such as what they like and dislike, how they look, behave or feel, etc.

On a piece of lined paper, have the children write the letters of their name vertically, placing one letter at the beginning of each line. The first letter of each name goes on the first line, the second letter goes on the next line and so on. If the name is short, they might want to use their middle or last name as well.

The children can fill in each line with a word or phrase that tells something about them, starting with the letter at the beginning of each line.

### Example:

**S** wimmer
**A** sker of questions
**L** ively
**L** ikes animals
**Y** ellow is my favourite colour

**B** anana eater
**R** uns fast
**O** wns a bird
**W** ears sandals
**N** eat

## My Name

The children can discover the unique visual representation of their name.

## Materials:

- construction paper
- scissors
- coloured crayons or markers
- pencils
- ruler

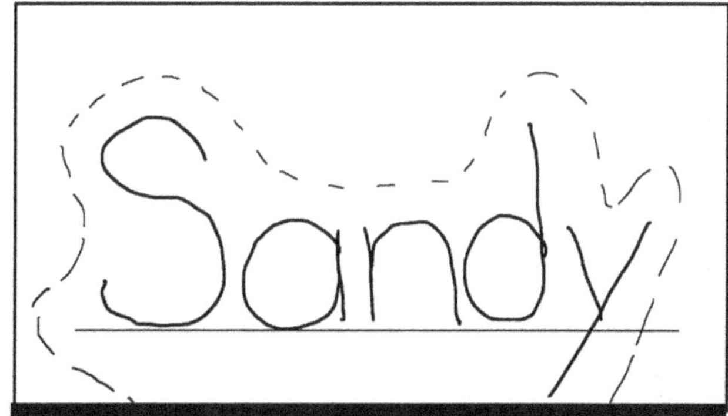
Cut on dotted line and unfold

## Procedure:

Have the children fold the sheet of construction paper in half lengthwise.

With the ruler draw a horizontal line 2cm (1 inch) above the fold.

Ask the children to write their name, or the name of a character from a story, on the line.

Draw around the letters of the name.

Cut along the line drawn around the letters, without disturbing the fold.

Open the cut out name and examine the shape.

With crayons or markers, transform the name into an animal, creature or art design of your choosing.

## Variation:

The children can cut out the spaces inside any loops, such as in a's or o's etc.

They can also mount their cut-out name on a contrasting piece of coloured paper.

You can talk to the children about the design of their name by asking such questions as: What does the shape make you think of? What does the shape remind you of?

# Prediction Activities

## Fortune Cookies or Fortune Cakes

You can bake cookies, cupcakes or a cake.

Prepare your fortunes on cut pieces of paper.

For fun you can place the fortunes into little plastic toys.

You can wrap each fortune-filled toy in tin foil or parchment paper and place the bundle into the cookie dough or into cake or cupcake batter.

It's fun for the children to learn to bake and to find their fortunes.

*When I was a child I remember a friend's birthday cake that was filled with fun surprises in every slice.*

## Astrology

Every child has a birthday and every birthdate has an astrological sign associated with it. It can be fun to let the children discover their astrological sign and find out some of the characteristics of that sign.

These Astrology Charts can be used to collect and record the children's names by their astrological sign to see which signs are most represented in the class.

Here is a list of the astrological signs with their dates, symbols, and a brief account of their attributes.

This is just for fun.

# Astrology Chart

| Sign | Meaning | Children |
|------|---------|----------|
| ♈ | Aries<br>(March 21 – April 20)<br>the Ram<br><br>Aries children enjoy adventure and leadership. | |
| ♉ | Taurus<br>(April 21 – May 21)<br>the Bull<br><br>Taurus children are reasonable, practical and determined. | |
| ♊ | Gemini<br>(May 22 – June 21)<br>the Twins<br><br>Gemini children are social butterflies and love to learn new things. | |
| ♋ | Cancer<br>(June 22 – July 22)<br>the Crab<br><br>Cancer children are sensitive, loving and have great memories. | |
| ♌ | Leo<br>(July 23 – August 22)<br>the Lion<br><br>Leo children love action and leadership. | |
| ♍ | Virgo<br>(August 23 – September 23)<br>the Virgin<br><br>Virgo children are shy, soft-hearted and strive for perfection. | |

# Astrology Chart

| Sign | Meaning | Children |
|---|---|---|
| ♎ | Libra<br>(September 24 – October 23)<br>the Scales<br><br>Libra children like to keep everything in a peaceful balance. | |
| ♏ | Scorpio<br>(October 24 – November 22)<br>the Scorpion<br><br>Scorpio children look for truth and justice. | |
| ♐ | Sagittarius<br>(November 23 – December 21)<br>the Archer<br><br>Sagittarius children are confident and adventurous. | |
| ♑ | Capricorn<br>(December 22 – January 20)<br>the Goat<br>Capricorn children are practical, stable and ambitious. | |
| ♒ | Aquarius<br>(January 21 – February 19)<br>the Water Bearer<br><br>Aquarius children are independent, friendly and march to the beat of their own drum. | |
| ♓ | Pisces<br>(February 20 – March 20)<br>the Fish<br><br>Pisces children are generous, sensitive and flow with the currents. | |

## Paper Fortune Tellers

**Template**

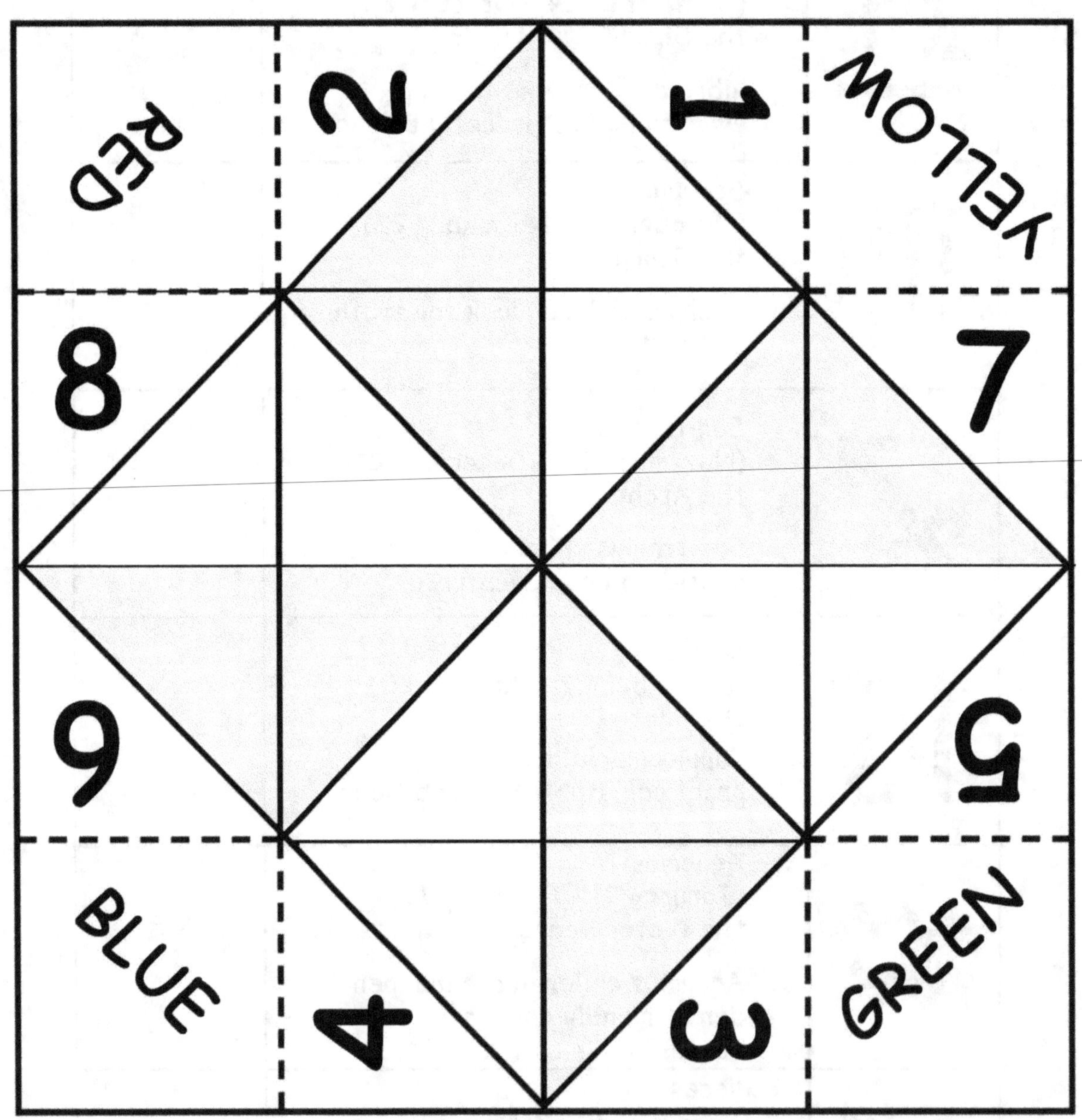

# How to make a Fortune Teller

Start with a sheet of paper

Fold up the corner to meet the other side

Fold up the other corner to meet the other side

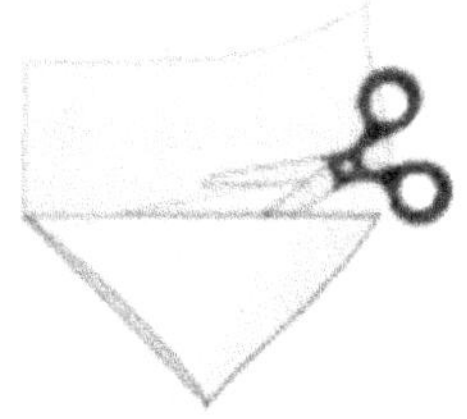

Cut off the top

Unfold to reveal a square

Fold all four corners so the points meet in the middle

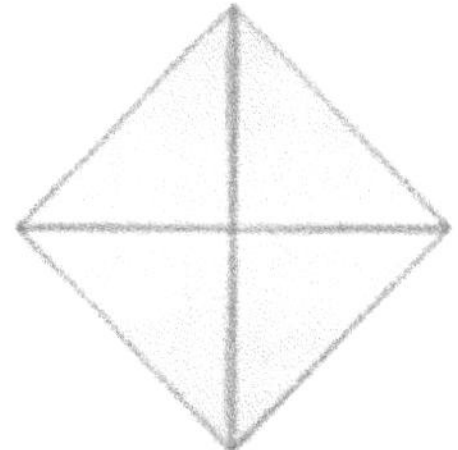

It should look like this

Flip it over

Fold up all four corners so the points meet in the middle

It should look like this

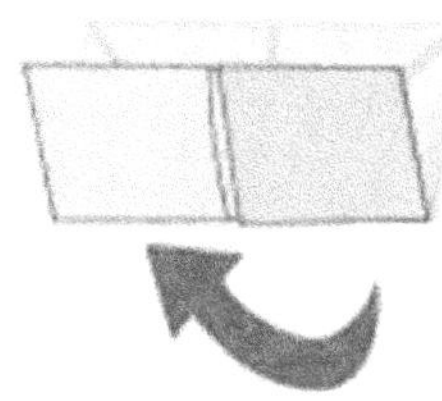

Fold

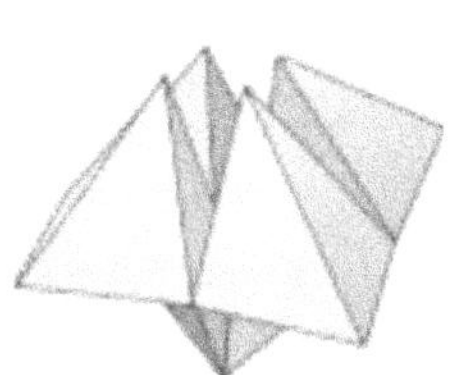

Work your fingers into the four corners

## Retell the Story

This activity is great for developing linear thinking.

Have the children talk about the timeless tale you are reading and ask them to retell it in chronological order. You can create a game of it by having one child begin the tale and retell the first event, have the next child recall the second event and continue the retelling until the class has reached the end of the story.

You can also retell or reread the story. Before you continue to read or tell the next event, you can ask the children if anyone knows what happens next.

This activity can go hand in hand with the activity "Timeline."

## Timeline

This activity is a visual representation of the sequential order of events of a story. Depending on the age or ability of your class, the children can write the events in words or illustrate the events in pictures or symbols on the timeline or the comic strip.

# Timeline

Ending

Beginning

# Comic Strip

# What's on My Mind?

"Who are you?" said the Caterpillar.
This was not an encouraging opening for a conversation. Alice
replied, rather shyly, "I—I hardly know, Sir, just at present—at
least I know who I was when I got up this morning, but I think I
must have been changed several times since then."
(Lewis Carroll, 1865, *Alice in Wonderland*)

In this activity the children will have the chance to think about
and examine their own unique ideas and preferences, such as,
things they like or would like to have; places they have been or
would like to go to; people they admire; books, movies, and apps
they enjoy, etc.

This is a visual representation of their own unique ideas which
answers the question, "What's on my mind?"

## Materials:

- Old magazines or printouts of photos, comic books, cartoons,
  advertisements, and so on
- Scissors and glue
- Cardboard and crayons or markers

## Procedure:

Ask the children to think about what is on their mind or the mind
of a story character.

The children can draw and cut out a silhouette of their own or
of a story character's profile. You can also provide ready-made
profiles to the children.

The profile will be the background for their own or their story
character's thoughts and ideas.

The children can draw, cut and paste a collage or write about
what is on their mind or the story character's mind.

# Wishing

Dictionaries define "wishes" as expressions of desires and hopes that are improbable or impossible.

You can ask the children what wishes are and where they think wishes come from.

You can ask what they would wish for if they were granted three wishes.

Questions such as:

- If you were granted three wishes what would they be? Why?
- If you were granted three wishes for someone else, what would they be? Why?
- If you could relive a day in your life, which day would you choose.
- Did you ever have a wish come true?
- What do you like about wishes?
- Where do you think wishes come from?

# Word Power

> Words are, in my not-so-humble opinion, our most inexhaustible source of magic...
> (J.K. Rowling, 1997, *Harry Potter and the Philosopher's Stone*)

Words have power. Even though children communicate a great deal without words, verbal expression is most important for building the mind's ideas and expressing them to others.

Exploring language can be fun and empowering for children. Learning interesting, unusual words and phrases sharpens the intellect and enhances the children's expression and listening skills. They can begin to explore and examine how their new vocabulary matches up with their intended meaning.

There are so many ways of using and choosing words. Some words make children feel powerful, some keep them out of trouble, sometimes sprinkling a little sugar on their words will sweeten what they want to say and sometimes a properly selected word can turn a friend's frown upside down.

What is most important is that children become aware of the power of words. Through awareness, children become clearer about who they are, what they want to say, how they want to say it and how they want their words to be understood. In this way they become aware of taking both the speaker and the listener into consideration.

Words are fun. Words are like magic. Words are a kind of superpower. And who doesn't want a superpower?

## Animated Words

You can ask the children to draw the meaning of a word using the letters that make up that word.

Animated words are lovely visual representations of words and their meanings.

## Big Words

**Sesquipedalian (ses-kwi-pi-dey-lee-uhn)**
- characterized by the use of long words with many syllables
- comes from Latin, meaning "a foot and a half"

**Sesquipedalian words** can be fun to use in spelling bees, word studies and vocabulary development. They enhance listening and pronunciation skills as well. The children can enjoy the challenge of learning new and unusual words and their meanings, as they try to figure out how these words relate to the timeless tales.

When I was an elementary school teacher I used to love to present my class with unusual and funny words. It always made me smile when I would hear any of my students try to incorporate a sesquipedalian word in their every-day language. Here are some for you and the children to have fun with.

**anthropomorphism (an-thruh-puh-mawr-fiz-uhm)**
- the attribution of human characteristics or behaviours to an animal or object

**befuddle (bih-fuhd-l)**
- unable to think clearly
- to confuse, perplex, bewilder, baffle or muddle

**bombastic (bom-bas-tik)**
- saying something important sounding with no real meaning
- pompous, grandiose, pretentious

**boondoggle (boon-dog-uhl)**
- an unnecessary, wasteful or fraudulent project or activity often involving graft

**Brobdingnagian (Brob-ding-nag-ee-uhn)**
- gigantic, huge, of immense proportions
- *Brobdingnag* is the imaginary land of giants in *Gulliver's Travels*, by Jonathan Swift. It is always written with a "B."

**cachinnate (kak-uh-neyt)**
- to laugh loudly or excessively

**circumlocution (sir-kuhm-loh-kyoo-shuhn)**
- The use of lots of words where fewer words would do, especially in a deliberate attempt to be vague or evasive.

**consequential (kon-si-kwen-shuhl)**
- following as an effect, as a result of or outcome

**contemporaneous (kuh n-tem-puh-rey-nee-uhs)**
- living or occurring during the same period of time
- two things happening at the same time

**cryptozoology (krip-toh-zoh-ol-uh-jee)**
- The search for and study of animals whose existence or survival is disputed or unsubstantiated, such as the Loch Ness monster and the yeti.

**disadvantageous (dis-ad-vuh n-tey-juhs)**
- creating unfavourable circumstances that reduce the chances of success or effectiveness

**discombobulate (dis-kuhm-bob-yuh-leyt)**
- to confuse someone or make someone feel uncomfortable

**dollop (dol-uh p)**
- refers to a shapeless mass, lump or blob of some substance
- in reference to food it is adding something casually

**euphemism (yoo-fuh-miz-uhm)**
- The substitution of a mild or inoffensive expression for one that may offend, embarrass or suggest something unpleasant.

**extemporaneous (eks-tem-puh-rey-nee-uhs)**
- spoken or done without preparation
- uttered on the spur of the moment

**facetious (fah-see-shuhs)**
- joking or jesting inappropriately
- treating a serious matter with inappropriate remarks, jokes or humour

**flabbergast (flab-er-gast)**
- to overwhelm with shock, surprise or amazement

**gasconade (gas-kuh-neyd)**
  • extravagant boasting or bragging

**hodgepodge (hoj-poj)**
  • a confused mixture of different things

**hullabaloo (huhl-uh-buh-loo)**
  • a commotion or a fuss

**humongous (hyoo-muhng-guhs)**
  • huge, enormous, extraordinarily large

**idiosyncrasy (id-ee-oh-sin-kruh-see)**
  • a characteristic mode of behaviour or way of thought that is peculiar to an individual

**incomprehensible (in-kom-pri-hen-suh-buhl)**
  • not able to understand or comprehend, unintelligible

**nincompoop (nin-kuh m-poop)**
  • a foolish or stupid person

**ornery (awr-nuh-ree)**
  • bad tempered or difficult to deal with

**pandemonium (pan-duh-moh-nee-uhm)**
  • wild and noisy disorder or confusion, an uproar

**phantasmagorical (fan-taz-muh-gawr-i-kuhl)**
  • a fantastical appearance, as something in a dream or created by the imagination

**quintessential (kwin-teh-sen-shul)**
  • representing the most perfect or typical example of something

**widdershins (with-er-shinz)**
  • counter-clockwise or anti-clockwise, describing the opposite direction from the way a clock moves
  • in the opposite or contrary direction from usual

**zenith (zee-nith)**
  • highest point, topmost, peak, apex, summit

## Sesquipedalian Phrases

The children in my elementary class always enjoyed the challenging game of working out sesquipedalian phrases. The children would sit in groups with a few dictionaries as they tried to work out the meanings of the common sayings. Some of the children memorized the sayings and would actually use them in the correct context. The first example I showed them was the one below, for obvious reasons.

The exuberance of your verbosity is too copious for my diminutive comprehension.
(meaning) *The words you are speaking are too large for my small understanding.*

Provide the children with paper dictionaries, or computers or tablets with access to online dictionaries. See if they can figure out the following common expressions.

1. Members of an avian species with identical plumage will congregate.
   (meaning: *Birds of a feather flock together.*)
2. Surveillance should precede saltation.
   (meaning: *Look before you leap.*)
3. Pulchritude possesses solely cutaneous profundity.
   (meaning: *Beauty is only skin deep.*)
4. It is futile to become lachrymose over precipitately departed lacteal fluids.
   (meaning: *Don't cry over spilled milk.*)
5. Freedom from incrustations of grime is contiguous to asceticism.
   (meaning: *Cleanliness is next to godliness.*)
6. The stylus is more potent than the dirk.
   (meaning: *The pen is mightier than the sword.*)
7. It is fruitless to indoctrinate a superannuated canine with innovative maneuvers.
   (meaning: *You can't teach an old dog new tricks.*)

8. The temperature of aqueous content of an unremittingly ogled culinary vessel does not attain caloric effervescence.
   (meaning: *A watched pot never boils.*)

9. All articles which coruscate with resplendence are not truly auriferous.
   (meaning: *All that glitters is not gold.*)

10. Missiles of ligneous or petrous consistency have the potential of fracturing my osseous structure, but appellations will remain sempiternally innocuous.
    (meaning: *Sticks and stones can break my bones, but names will never hurt me.*)

11. Individuals who make their abode in vitreous edifices would be advised to refrain from catapulting projectiles.
    (meaning: *People who live in glass houses shouldn't throw stones.*)

12. Never venture to prognosticate upon the younger generation of poultry until the final process of incubation has been exercised.
    (meaning: *Don't count your chickens until they are hatched.*)

13. Neophyte's serendipity.
    (meaning: *Beginner's luck.*)

14. The person presenting the ultimate cachinnation possesses thereby the optimal cachinnation.
    (meaning: *He who laughs last, laughs best.*)

15. If an enclosure for a pedal extremity adapts itself suitably to said appendage, it would be advisable to employ it accordingly.
    (meaning: *If the shoe fits, wear it.*)

16. No individual specimen in the species Homo Sapiens exists in a condition of isolation.
    (meaning: *No man is an island.*)

All the world's a stage,
And all the men and women merely players;
They have their exits and their entrances,
And one man in his time plays many parts,
(William Shakespeare, 1623, *As You Like It*, 2·7)

# Part 2

## The Play of Words, Implementation

# The Play of Knowledge, Gyan Yoga

One of the hardest things in the world is to convey a meaning accurately from one mind to another.
(Lewis Carroll, 1865, *Alice In Wonderland*)

This is where everything comes together—where the philosophical knowledge, practical skills and terminology unite with the wisdom of the *Timeless Tales* to form an organic whole, under the umbrella of each story theme.

These charming treasures, in the shape of inspiring stories, stir and stretch the imagination, sharpen the intellect and delight the mind. They also provide a marvellous basis for discussions on so many levels and in so many ways as the children explore and examine the unique warp and weft of each enchanting tale. As the children listen to the unravelling of each tale they can close their eyes in meditation or just sit back and enjoy the play of words.

These *Timeless Tales* present extraordinary opportunities for children to grow and develop. Through the practice of meditation, guided discussions, yoga disciplines and activities, the development of the whole child is enriched and refined. Watching children blossom into their own very best self is really magical. And this is where it happens.

These stories can be read and reread over and over and over again because each and every reading reveals layers of depth, meaning and delight. Thoughtful discussions that spark the mind and develop higher levels of thinking skills encourage children to explore the deeper interpretations of the story themes. A meaningful foundation for communication is cultivated as the sense of ease in handling language develops. In this way the children learn to clarify their expression as they unite their thoughts and ideas with their words.

These insightful stories are not listed in any particular order, which means you can select a story randomly or according to the suitability of its topic. Each story has a specific significant theme. To explore the theme a comprehensive curricular lesson is coupled with each tale. Every lesson offers suggestions and methods on how to implement, enrich and explore the essence of each story theme. The story-messages are so potent that several classes can be spent on a single tale. Sometimes you may revisit a story at a later date because of its relevance to a particular life situation that may come up in the class.

All the lessons provide a well-rounded, meaningful foundation for growth and expansion in meditation and yoga disciplines, communication and learning-centred skills and activities, which can be practiced individually or shared by the group as a whole. Use as much or as little of the suggested material as you like. You can choose, use and adapt the activities and materials to suit the ages, needs, temperaments, learning styles and abilities of your class children.

## Getting Started

There are many different ways to begin a class. The material provided in "The Lesson" supplies the theme of each story, suggested discussion ideas and questions, theme-related approaches to meditation and the yoga disciplines as well as fun games and activities that relate to the theme of each story. With "The Lesson" in mind, I have offered some suggestions on ways to begin a class.

You can begin a class by reading a story straight away. Often I enjoyed starting a class this way. It fascinated me to observe the changes in perception and understanding in both the children and myself after we had explored many aspects of the story's topic. When I would reread the story I would observe how we all listened with fresh ears.

Alternatively, a class could begin with suggested hatha yoga poses and meditation practices; including pranayama and mantra. These activities are always a great way to begin a session with children. They settle their energy and provide a readiness for tuning in to the stories.

A third approach would be to begin a class by asking questions that directly relate to the theme of the story you are going to read. A list of suggested discussion questions is provided in "The Lesson." You can ask, "Does anyone know what certain words mean?" or "Has anyone ever felt like this?" These kinds of discussion questions pique the interest of children and familiarize them with the theme of the story before the initial reading.

The questions provided in "The Lessons" are helpful guidelines to lead the students' attention to their own understanding of the topics presented. When discussing personal experiences and how children feel or perceive them, there usually are no right or wrong answers. It is a time for exploration and expression, where the children should feel free to express, communicate and examine their thoughts and ideas in a safe environment. With your guidance, they can recognize and observe the changing nature of the mind and become aware of the one who is watching it, the unchanging observer, the Knower.

Presenting dictionary definitions in the form of questions and discussions serves as a common ground for understanding and a great starting place for discussions. Playing with words and their meanings offers children the chance to explore and learn about language and communication skills while they practice articulating their thoughts and ideas and probe deeper meanings.

When you start with a discussion before reading the story, then after hearing the story and completing several exercises, you can ask the children if they notice any changes in their thinking on the topic.

It is important for children to be reminded of the changing nature of the mind and to understand that it is totally natural for people to change their minds, their points of view and their thinking when new information is provided. It is the nature of the mind to change in order to greet the new input of information. The one inside you who knows that the mind is always changing remains the same, forever unchanging. That is you, the Knower.

> But words are things, and a small drop of ink,
> Falling like dew, upon a thought, produces
> That which makes thousands, perhaps millions, think.
> (Lord Byron, 1819, *Don Juan*)

I can still remember sitting with friends and colleagues, listening with rapt attention to the enchanting words of my teacher, Swami Shyam. His captivating style of storytelling always delighted us, as he unravelled his tales filled with the eternal wisdom of the ages. He showered his profound knowledge in the form of delight, informing us that delight was always a quality of higher knowledge.

These timeless tales will enchant, delight and unite the story with the storyteller and the story listeners.

Enjoy!

# Timeless Tales and Their Lessons


1. Cunning Mr Monkey
2. Destiny
3. Donkey Riding
4. Fox and Camel
5. Kalpataru
6. The Bribe
7. The Self Fish
8. Truth Story
9. What Is an Elephant?

# Timeless Tale 1
# Cunning Mr Monkey

Two cats came across one great big loaf of bread. She Cat wanted the loaf all for herself and He Cat wanted the loaf all for himself. Both cats were very greedy and very selfish and they began to quarrel with each other.

Just then cunning Mr Monkey came along and saw the two cats quarrelling. Mr Monkey said, "Why are you cats quarrelling? What is the matter?"

She Cat said, "Well, there is only one loaf and I want it all for myself."

He Cat said, "There is only one loaf and I want it all for myself."

Mr Monkey, who was very clever and cunning and equally as greedy and selfish, thought that he too would like to have that loaf of bread all for himself. He sat quietly observing the greedy behaviour of the cats, and devised a plan in his mind to obtain the whole loaf for himself.

Mr Monkey spoke to the cats. He said, "Now look, you are two cats and there is one loaf. It should be shared by both of you. It should be shared half and half."

The cats listened carefully to the logic of Mr Monkey. Then He Cat said, "You are right. It should be shared, but she wants more than me."

She Cat said, "No, he wants more than me." Then the two cats again began to quarrel.

In order to calm them down Mr Monkey declared, "With this kind of attitude there is bound to be trouble. You should put me in charge."

The two cats, who could never agree on anything, agreed to put Mr Monkey in charge.

Mr Monkey told the cats that he was going to cut the loaf in half so there would be two pieces of bread of equal size. He told them that each would have a piece of bread that would be the exact same size as the other. In this way, He Cat and She Cat would share the loaf of bread equally.

*Cunning Mr Monkey was hatching his plan to swindle the two cats out of the loaf of bread.*

Mr Monkey got a great big knife and cut the loaf in half. But cunning Mr Monkey didn't cut it exactly in half. Mr Monkey cut one side bigger and one side smaller.

Mr Monkey examined the two parts of the loaf and told He Cat and She Cat that in order to make sure that both cats were going to get exactly the same size piece, he would have to weigh the two pieces of bread on a scale.

Mr Monkey got a scale and hung it from a nearby tree. He carefully placed the bigger piece on one side and the smaller piece on the other. The cats watched as the side with the bigger piece went down and the side with the smaller piece went up.

Mr Monkey carefully examined the two pieces of bread on either side of the scale. He told He Cat and She Cat that the loaf was not cut evenly. He said that in order to make the two pieces even, he needed to cut off a piece from the bigger half of the loaf, thus reducing the size of the bigger piece to make it the same size as the smaller piece.

He Cat and She Cat attentively watched the procedure to make sure that each of them would receive an equal piece from the loaf. They watched in anticipation as Mr Monkey carefully cut from the bigger piece of bread...and ate the piece he cut off.

Mr Monkey who was very clever and cunning, cut so much off from the bigger piece, that the bigger piece became smaller and the smaller piece became bigger...and the two cats were watching, waiting.

Mr Monkey continued to even out the loaf as he ate the bits and pieces of bread that he cut from each side, while the cats sat watching.

In the end cunning Mr Monkey ate the whole loaf of bread all by himself. The cats never had the chance to get any at all.

# The Lesson
## Cunning Mr Monkey

## Theme

This adorable little tale demonstrates the wit and ingenuity of cunning Mr Monkey. The story begins with two cats who, out of their greed and selfishness, are unwilling to share a loaf of bread. They meet Mr Monkey, who hides his own greed and selfishness, and uses his cleverness and cunning to swindle the cats out of the whole loaf of bread right before their eyes.

In life, such things happen to almost everyone at one time or another. This story is a simple reminder to keep your eye on the goal, remain alert and know that sometimes you may end up putting your trust in someone, like Mr Monkey, who doesn't have your best interest at heart. You have to remain alert and aware of your own best interest.

The mind is constantly changing, bringing all manner of challenges to our lives. If we take a moment to pause, close our eyes in meditation and focus on the unchanging Knower that is always there, clarity and strength will be revealed.

## Discussion

When there is a dispute, sometimes the children involved lose focus and forget what they are fighting about. The cats got distracted by Mr Monkey's antics and forgot that they were fighting with each other over a loaf of bread. He Cat and She

Cat became distracted and listened to the cunning wiles of Mr Monkey, who was interested in having the loaf all for himself, and in the end, he did. When the cats lost their focus they also lost their goal—the loaf of bread.

It's curious to observe that the loss of focus distracted the cats so much, that they forgot about their fight with each other. Instead, they sat watching as cunning Mr Monkey ate the entire loaf of bread, piece by piece, right in front of their eyes.

I remember when I was a child, my best friend's mother had a policy for sharing. Her mother would give us a piece of cake to share. The rule was, one cut and the other one got first pick.

## Dictionary Meanings

It's always great to discuss and have fun with words and their meanings. Below are the dictionary definitions of some pertinent words in this story.

**cunning:**
- The ability to achieve things in a clever way, often by trickery or deceit.

**selfish:**
- someone who puts their own interests before others, only thinking of their own advantage
- lacking consideration for other people

**share:**
- to divide things
- to assume something in common
- to use something at the same time as someone else

**swindle:**
- to obtain by fraud, deceit or dishonesty

**alertness:**
- the quality of being aware and attentive
- a state of readiness to respond

This story can be a lot of fun to talk about, discuss and even re-enact as an impromptu play.

It is important to keep alert and focussed on your goal. When you pay attention to the one who is observing the goal, wisdom is developed. The one who is observing and knowing the goal is you, the Knower.

## Suggested Discussion Questions

- What is the story about?
- Has something like this ever happened to you or someone you know?
- What does the word "cunning" mean?
- What does the word "selfishness" mean?
- What does the word "share" mean?
- What does the word "swindle" mean?
- What does the word "alertness" mean?
- How would you share a bowl of popcorn, a piece of cake, cookies or candies?
- How would you share time on a game, on an app, or with a pet?
- What plan did Mr Monkey devise to have the loaf of bread all for himself?
- What would you have done?
- Why do you think the cats just sat there watching the monkey eat the bread?
- Who do you think was the most greedy and selfish—He Cat, She Cat or Mr Monkey? Why?
- How can you keep your attention on your goal?
- What happens to He Cat, She Cat, Mr Monkey and the loaf of bread when you are asleep?

- Who is always there observing and listening as the story is being told?

# Meditation

## Mantra Meditation

The two cats could have had some tips on maintaining alertness when cunning Mr Monkey came along. Mantra meditation helps to focus the mind and develop alertness. You can begin to introduce the mantra *Shyām* or *Om* by giving its meaning as well as its correct pronunciation (please refer to the chapter, The Play of Sound, Mantra). Or you can introduce other mantras such as "be alert" or "focus, focus, focus." Start by repeating the mantra aloud and ask the children to chime in. Slowly make your voice quieter and quieter as the children follow your lead. Finally ask them to continue repeating the mantra inside.

## Mala Meditation

Some children may like to use a mala during mantra meditation as it provides tactile concentration and focus. (See mala in The Play of Action, Karma Yoga.)

# The Play of Breath, Pranayama

Specific instructions on how to perform the breath exercises are found in the chapter "The Play of Breath, Pranayama."

## Awareness of the Movement of Breath
## प्राण चिन्तन प्राणायाम Prān Chintan Prānāyām

This exercise is wonderful for developing awareness as well as finding out your own pattern and rhythm of breathing. The cats would have been more alert had they remembered to practice this exercise.

## Abdominal Breathing अधम प्राणायाम Adham Prānāyām

Ask the children to locate their natural breath with their fingers. They will most likely, point to the chest area. Then ask them to place their fingers on the tummy area—where the loaf of bread ended up in Mr Monkey—and breathe into where their fingers are. They can imagine that their breath is reaching the loaf of bread.

## Alternate Nostril Breathing
## अनुलोम-विलोम प्राणायाम Anulom-Vilom Prānāyām

You can have fun with this exercise by telling the children that they can unite He Cat and She Cat as friends in breath. Ask them to inhale to He and pause to Cat, then exhale to She and pause to Cat. As they continue this exercise the children will come to see that the movement of their breath—inhale to He, exhale to She—changes. When they pause to Cat, that is where He Cat and She Cat are united. They are united in the unchanging pause (paws) of the Knower.

## Balanced Breathing
## सम-वृत्ति प्राणायाम Sam-Vritti Prānāyām

In this balanced breathing exercise, or square pattern, you can call each of the four parts characters from the story. With equal timings the children can inhale to He Cat, pause to Mr Monkey, exhale to She Cat and pause to the loaf of bread.

## Shining Forehead
## कपालभाति प्राणायाम Kapālbhāti Prānāyām

This exercise is called shining forehead and is said to illuminate the mind. This is a great exercise for those who would like to avoid being swindled out of their loaf of bread.

# The Play of Sound, Mantra

Information and specific instructions on pronunciation of mantras are found in the chapter "The Play of Sound, Mantra."

## Amaram Hum Madhuram Hum अमरम् हं मधुरम् हं

Those who repeat this beautiful mantra will never lose their piece of bread—or peace of mind—because *Amaram Hum Madhuram Hum* keeps you and your mind alert.

## Om ॐ

The universal sound of *Om* develops focus and alertness. If He Cat and She Cat had repeated this mantra they would have figured out a way to share that loaf of bread.

## Om Shānti ॐ शान्ति

This mantra invokes the sense of peace. The children can observe the interesting circumstances that the cats and the monkey found themselves in, and how it might have been different had they repeated *Om Shānti Shānti Shānti*.

## Shiv शिव

The mantra *Shiv* is said to bring happiness and the sense of being undisturbed by disappearance. This would be a great mantra for He Cat and She Cat to repeat. I think Mr Monkey must have repeated it when he met the cats and first laid eyes on that loaf of bread.

## Shyām श्याम

This mantra represents the blue-black space that is untouched by the world. The mantra *Shyām* carries the sense of watchful appreciation to the children as they come to enjoy and value all the characters in the story and the parts they play that make the story unique and fun to listen to.

## Mantras of your own choosing

The children can come up with a variety of fun mantras for this story such as "Me me me me me." In how many languages can you say "Me?"

# The Play of Body, Hatha Yoga

Specific instructions on how to perform the poses can be found in the chapter "The Play of Body, Hatha Yoga."

## Cat Poses मार्जरीआसन/बिडालासन Mārjārīāsan/Bidālāsan

The children can play the roles of She Cat (*mārjārī*) and He Cat (*bidāl*) as they perform the two parts of this pose.

## Tree Pose वृक्षासन Vrikshāsan

When Mr Monkey wanted to check if he had cut the loaf exactly in half, he got a scale and hung it from a tree. The children can pose as that tree.

## Equestrian Pose अश्व सञ्चलनासन Ashwa Sanchalanāsan

The children can perform the equestrian pose and instead of being a horse they can pretend to be cunning Mr Monkey.

## Lion Pose सिंघासन Singhāsan

A lion is also a cat that is often referred to as the king of the jungle. I wonder what kind of cunning antics Mr Monkey would come up with to distract a lion.

## Downward-Facing Dog Pose अधोमुखश्वानासन Adho Mukh Shwānāsan

The children might wonder how the cats felt as they watched the entire loaf of bread being eaten by cunning Mr Monkey, right before their eyes. It might be like a downward-facing dog. The great thing about this pose is that it is both invigorating and rejuvenating.

## Child Pose बालासन Bālāsan

In this relaxing, restful pose the children can imagine they are the loaf of bread baking in the oven.

# The Play of Action, Karma Yoga

The instructions for these activities can be found in the chapter "The Play of Action, Karma Yoga."

## Balance Scales

The children can have fun learning how to make a balance scale. They can also play with the scale the way Mr Monkey did. You can give the children objects to divvy up with their friends on the balance scales.

## Back-to-Back Communication

The two cats could have done well with this fun-filled communication activity. The children can be He Cat and She Cat learning to communicate with each other.

## Commercials

The children can make commercials on topics such as how to remain alert under all circumstances, how to be clever and cunning or how to share things with friends.

## Word Power

Words are like a superpower. It's always great to have a superpower.

**Animated Words**: The children can animate words from the story such as cat, monkey, loaf of bread or more challenging words such as share and cunning.

**Big Words**: Playing with big words is always a lot of fun. Here are some **sesquipedalian words** to go with the story.

**anthropomorphism (an-thruh-puh-mawr-fiz-uhm)**
- the attribution of human characteristics or behaviours to an animal or object

**befuddle (bih-fuhd-l)**
- unable to think clearly
- to confuse, perplex, bewilder, baffle or muddle

**consequential (kon-si-kwen-shuhl)**
- following as an effect, as a result of or outcome

**discombobulate (dis-kuhm-bob-yuh-leyt)**
- to confuse someone or make someone feel uncomfortable

**extemporaneous (eks-tem-puh-rey-nee-uhs)**
- spoken or done without preparation
- uttered on the spur of the moment

**flabbergast (flab-er-gast)**
- to overwhelm with shock, surprise or amazement

**nincompoop (nin-kuh m-poop)**
- a foolish or stupid person

Here are some **sesquipedalian phrases** to go with the story.

The person presenting the ultimate cachinnation possesses thereby the optimum cachinnation.
(meaning: *He who laughs last, laughs best.*)

It is futile to become lachrymose over precipitately departed lacteal fluids.
(meaning: *Don't cry over spilled milk.*)

Never venture to prognosticate upon the younger generation of poultry until the final process of incubation has been exercised.
(meaning: *Don't count your chickens until they are hatched.*)

## What's on My Mind?

The children can create a silhouette of one of the characters from the story. On the silhouette they can draw, or cut and paste, what they think was going on in the mind of that character.

## Building Bridges

Sometimes the sense of cooperation is called for. This bridge building activity is just that.

# Timeless Tale 2
# Destiny

*Destiny belongs to the body. Whether the daughter of a king is destined to marry the son of a chimney sweep, or whether she is destined to marry a king, it will all happen according to her destiny. But remember, destiny belongs to the body.*

When a daughter was born to the king and queen of the continent, they asked their astrologer who she was going to marry.

The astrologer looked into the princess's future and came to see that she was going to marry the son of the king's chimney sweep, a boy who had recently been born in the king's court. With some trepidation the astrologer delivered the news to the king and queen.

Upon hearing this, the king flew into a rage. He would never permit his daughter to have such a marriage. He asked the astrologer how her destiny could be averted. The astrologer said, "That which is destined to happen, will happen. It is inevitable."

The king said, "Such a marriage can never take place. It must be averted."

The queen turned to her husband and said, "You must finish this little chimney sweep boy, and then there will be no question of this marriage ever happening."

But the king of the continent thought to challenge the astrologer's science, "I can alter our daughter's destiny. I can allow the chimney sweep boy to live and still see that this marriage does not happen. Then we will see about the astrologer's science of predictions."

The king was so sure of his own power that he made a wager with the astrologer, "I am sure that my daughter will never marry this chimney sweep boy. I will not allow it. After all, marriages are arranged by fathers and I will never allow such a marriage to take place."

The astrologer said, "Do whatever you like, but it is going to happen."

The king discussed the matter with his wife. They decided that this chimney sweep child should be thrown in the ocean. The king said, "If he is saved, then it is his destiny."

The queen considered the astrologer's claim on their daughter's destiny, "Suppose he is saved, how would we know for sure that he is the same chimney sweep boy?"

The king thought about this. He decided to have one of the boy's toes cut off, his big toe. The king called his henchman to his chambers and commanded him to cut off the young chimney sweep's big toe and then throw him in the ocean and leave him to his fate.

Thus, the chimney sweep boy was taken away and thrown into the ocean without his toe. In the water, however, the waves kept him afloat and soon a ship passed near him. Seeing the drowning little boy, the captain ordered his crew to rescue him. The boy was taken aboard the ship and they sailed across the ocean. When the ship reached a nice island, he was dropped off and the ship continued on its way.

Now, as it happened, or as it was his destiny, on this island the king had just died leaving no son, or heir to replace him. Everyone was waiting and wondering what to do. Then one of the ministers found written in their scriptures, that in such a case, someone from far away would be found on the sea beach, that very day. That someone would be made their king.

Thus, this chimney sweep boy was seated on the throne and crowned as king of the island kingdom. He was educated in all such manners and habits befitting a king. He learned their language, customs, cultures and laws, and his attire was always befitting the status of a king. Now, in this island country the custom was that the king always wore special foot coverings, or shoes, so that his toes were never visible. Nobody on the island kingdom knew that their king was missing his big toe. Slowly and slowly, the chimney sweep boy grew and became capable of ruling.

Many years passed and now the daughter of the king and queen of the continental kingdom reached marriageable age. So the king of the continent sent his men out to find a superfine husband, a king's son perhaps, to marry their daughter.

In their search for a fitting match, they found a young king from a distant island. The king and queen were pleased when they met the young king, and so allowed their daughter to meet him. She immediately fell in love and agreed to the marriage.

*Now who could ever think that the son of a chimney sweep could become a king?*

Certainly the king never did, nor did his queen. They were too busy making arrangements for the marriage party. A big celebration was planned with bands, lights, banners, canopies and all kinds of friends and celebrities were invited. The king was very happy because he believed he had averted the fate of his daughter who was destined to marry a chimney sweep.

When the marriage ceremony was over and they saw their daughter being carried in the palanquin, the king said to his wife, "Is it really possible that I have averted her destiny?"

"I just knew that astrologer could not figure out such things," the queen replied.

When the astrologer arrived at the wedding party the king said to him, "Well, what do you think of your science of astrology now? Tell me, where is my daughter's destiny? I'll tell you, I have succeeded in altering it. I have won."

The astrologer was quiet, what could he say? He could not think that this young king of the island kingdom, who had just married the king's daughter, was the son of the king's chimney sweep— the same little boy who was thrown in the ocean without his big toe. The astrologer just said, "Well, what can I say. This is what was written in her destiny. And it said that it will be met."

The king, feeling very sure of himself said, "Well, if it is so, then we should check to see if his big toe is missing."

So the king of the continent asked his daughter's new husband to take off his shoes. Now, the young king of the island did not know anything about the bet between the astrologer and the king of the continent. He was so young when this story began that he didn't know or remember the circumstances that brought him to the island kingdom where he was crowned the king. He did not want to remove his shoes because it was not the custom of the island kingdom to do so, and he was feeling shy about missing his big toe.

After the marriage ceremony everyone was invited for dinner inside the palace dining room. It was the custom in the continental kingdom that before eating, everyone must remove their shoes. And then the king, the queen and the astrologer saw that he had no big toe. But it was too late, they were already married.

*Now this explains destiny. But destiny belongs to the body...and never to you!*

# The Lesson
## Destiny

## Theme

In a lighthearted way, this story portrays destiny as that which is predetermined and inevitable. Playing with this concept, the story supports the claim that no matter what a person does to alter an outcome, what is meant to be, will be.

The most significant point of the story is that destiny belongs to the body. This means that the body is fixed to a situation or circumstance. As the story demonstrates, the king's daughter was destined to marry the son of the chimney sweep, and she did marry him in spite of her parents best efforts to avert her destiny. However, by the time she marries him, he has become a king in his own right.

Destiny belongs to the body and mind which is constantly changing. The Knower state represents the freedom that can play with the fixity of any destiny and make that destiny work for the person in the most marvellous of ways.

## Discussion

It is always great to talk with the children about what they have understood from the story and how they relate to what they have heard.

When children first hear this story their attention is drawn to the events. In order to probe deeper into the meaning—destiny belongs to the body—meditation is needed.

## Dictionary Meanings

Introducing relevant vocabulary words and their meanings provides a starting point for understanding. From this starting point, the children can build their listening, understanding and discussion skills.

**destiny:**
- a predetermined course of events that will happen in the future
- the hidden power believed to control future events, fate

William Shakespeare presented the notion of destiny as,

> It is not in the stars to hold our destiny but in ourselves.
> (William Shakespeare, 1599, *Julius Ceaser*, 1·2)

**prediction:**
- a forecast
- a statement about what will happen in the future

**astrology:**
- The study of the movements and relative positions of celestial bodies interpreted as having an influence on people, their lives and the natural world.

**astrologer:**
- A person who uses astrology to tell others about their character or predict their future.

This story shows that destiny belongs to the body. Despite his humble beginnings, the chimney sweep boy became a king and did indeed marry the daughter of the king of the continent as the astrologer had foreseen.

The children can learn that their predetermined destinies—their family, country, nationality, mother tongue, gender, health, eye colour, etc.—belong to the body. Perhaps a person can't change their destiny, but they certainly can make it work to their benefit.

Meditation and guided discussions can help reveal the source of everyone's destiny. That source is the Knower state of consciousness, and the Knower state will always work for you.

## Suggested Discussion Questions

- What does destiny mean?
- What are predictions?
- What is astrology?
- What is an astrologer?
- What happened to the chimney sweep boy? How did he end up becoming a king?
- What bet did the king make with the astrologer?
- What have you understood from the story? Can you relate to the story?
- Do you have a destiny? What would that be?
- What destinies, or predetermined conditions, are part of your life?
- What does it mean to be in charge of your destiny?
- Who is in charge of your destiny?
- What happens to your destiny when you are asleep?
- What does the statement "destiny belongs to the body" mean to you?

## Meditation

### Knower Meditation

The children can take a voyage through their own minds and thoughts. You can remind them that the one who is watching and knowing the mind and thoughts is their own Self, the Knower.

## Guided Meditation

You can reread the story as the children sit and meditate. Ask them to think about who is listening to the story? Who is knowing the events of the story? You can remind them that the one who is listening, knowing, watching and remembering is their own Self, the Knower.

## Mantra Meditation

The children can use a kingly mantra such as *Rām* or even the powerful line from the story "destiny belongs to the body." It can also be fun to have the children create their own mantras for meditation.

## Mala Meditation

If children are feeling fidgety, you can suggest that they repeat a mantra using the mala. They can say a mantra on each bead and continue until they come to the end of the string. I often suggest that children use a hand mala or a smaller number of beads. (see "Mala" in the chapter The Play of Action, Karma Yoga)

When using a mala the children can also use each bead as an event from the story, or as a step on their own journey to reach the Knower state.

# Play of Breath, Pranayama

Specific instructions on how to perform the breath exercises are found in the chapter "The Play of Breath, Pranayama."

## Abdominal Breathing अधम प्राणायाम Adham Prānāyām

This breath exercise provides the clarity, depth and calm that a person would need when they are learning to become a king.

## Alternate Nostril Breathing
## अनुलोम-विलोम प्राणायाम Anulom-Vilom Prāṇāyām

The meaning of this exercise is that it goes with the grain (*anulom*) and against the grain (*vilom*). It is like the bet that the king and his astrologer made with each other. When the children perform this exercise they can inhale to the prediction of the astrologer, pause, exhale to the king who was determined to change his daughter's destiny, pause, inhale to the prediction and so forth. The children can be reminded that the one who is breathing with the grain (*anulom*) and against the grain (*vilom*) is one and the same breather.

## Victory Breath or Ocean Breath
## उज्जायी प्राणायाम Ujjayī Prāṇāyām

This exercise symbolizes the sound of the ocean waves that kept the young chimney sweep boy afloat until the boat rescued him, and the victory he achieved in becoming king of the island country.

## Shining Forehead
## कपालभाति प्राणायाम Kapālbhāti Prāṇāyām

When the astrologer realized that he won the bet with his king, his forehead must have been shining with delight.

## Chanting Breath उद्गीथ प्राणायाम Udgīth Prāṇāyām

The children can celebrate the chimney sweep boy becoming king of the island country and marrying the princess. They can exhale the mantra *Om* or mantras of peace and love to celebrate their union.

## King of Pranayama
### केवल कुम्भक प्राणायाम Keval Kumbhak Prānāyām

The children can hold the pause between the inhalation and exhalation, just as the young chimney sweep had done when he was in the water before he was rescued. By holding the pause the chimney sweep boy became king of the island kingdom. The children who hold this pause will become a King of Pranayama.

# Play of Sound, Mantra

Information and specific instructions on pronunciation of mantras are found in the chapter "The Play of Sound, Mantra."

## Rām राम

*Rām* is a kingly mantra representing victory and success. It is a great mantra that will create a royal sense of positive self-esteem in the children.

## Jai Rām Shrī Rām जय राम श्री राम

This kingly mantra celebrates victory and achievement. When repeating this mantra the children can know that their destiny belongs to the body, but the one who is repeating it is their own Self, the Knower. This mantra can also be repeated as a chant.
*Jai Rām Shrī Rām Jai Jai Rām*
*Jai Rām Shrī Rām Jai Jai Rām*

## Hare Krishna Hare Rām हरे कृष्ण हरे राम

This mantra can be repeated by the children celebrating the chimney sweep boy who became a king. In this way the boy's destiny, which belonged to his body, was transformed. In the same way the children can transform their destiny, which belongs to their body, to one of joy, delight, peace and freedom.

This mantra found its way into popular culture with George Harrison's song "My Sweet Lord."

*Hare Krishna Hare Krishna, Krishna Krishna, Hare Hare*
*Hare Rām Hare Rām, Rām Rām, Hare Hare*

## Om Rām Shiv Shyām ॐ राम शिव श्याम

This mantra evokes peace, compassion, bliss and detachment. It could be repeated in celebration of the destiny that belongs to the body, remembering that the one repeating this mantra is you, the Knower.

## Mantras of your own choosing

You can ask the children think about what they would like their destiny to be and choose a mantra accordingly. They can choose interesting mantras from different languages. Mantra examples could be, "Peace, Happiness, Love" or "Destiny belongs to the body."

# Play of Body, Hatha Yoga

Specific instructions on how to perform the poses can be found in the chapter "The Play of Body, Hatha Yoga."

## Tree Pose वृक्षासन Vrikshāsan

You can ask the children to stand tall and focused, like the young chimney sweep boy who was transformed into a king. You can have the children pretend that the upper foot is the one without the big toe.

## Boat Poses नावासन Nāvāsan

The children can pretend to be in the boat that takes the chimney sweep boy across the ocean, without his toe.

## Bridge Pose सेतुबन्धसर्वाङ्गासन Setu Bandh Sarvāngāsan

This pose is like the bridge between the different life experiences that the chimney sweep boy encountered on his way to fulfilling his destiny of marrying the king's daughter.

## Sphinx Pose सलम्ब भुजङ्गासन Salamb Bhujangāsan

This is a supported cobra pose. The children can think of the support the young chimney sweep boy had when he was being prepared to become king of the island country. We can all use a little support sometimes.

## Warrior Poses वीरभद्रासन Vīrabhadrāsan

When the chimney sweep boy was training to be king, he would have been taught to be a warrior as well. The children can hold these poses as masterful warriors.

## Lion Pose सिंघासन Singhāsan

The lion is known as the king of the jungle. In this pose the children can pretend to be the king who was furious to think that his daughter was going to marry the son of the king's chimney sweep. The children can roar at the astrologer.

## Sun Salutation Poses सूर्यनमस्कारासन Sūrya Namaskārāsan

This series of poses takes the children on a voyage of destiny as they start with the mountain pose and end with the mountain pose. In the same way, the chimney sweep boy started and ended up in the same kingdom where he had begun. Performing the sun salutation can be transformative for the children who perform it.

# The Play of Action, Karma Yoga

The instructions for these activities can be found in the chapter "The Play of Action, Karma Yoga."

## Retell the Story

Retell the Story is a fabulous activity as it takes the children on a voyage from here to there and back again. The teacher can begin by recalling how the story began and have the children, in turn, see if they can recall what comes next, until they reach the end of the story. This activity is great for developing linear thinking.

## Timeline

This activity helps develop linear thinking. The children can create a visual representation of the sequence of events. They can use the timeline or the comic strip. In this way they recall the events in order of occurrence. It can be done in conjunction with "Retell the Story," which is a discussion activity.

## Compass and Mapmaking Skills

A compass helps people find their way and guide them to their destinations. Learning to make a compass can be an engaging activity for children as they set sail on their own adventures.

You can use old maps or have the children draw their own, making sure to place North, South, East, West on the map so the children can use their compass to navigate to different destinations. Using old maps, or maps of their own making, they can chart the sea voyage of the chimney sweep boy, from the kingdom of his birth to the island kingdom and back again.

## Prediction Games and Astrology Chart

The children can have fun and become familiar with astrology, the method of prediction in this story. There are also a number of prediction games included in this section, from paper fortune tellers to fortune cookies. You can also discuss such things as weather forecasts, the value of predictions and how they are made.

## Coat of Arms

Every kingdom has their own coat of arms. It can be fun for the children to create one that represents who they are, or you can have them create a coat of arms for the kingdom of the king and queen or the island kingdom of the sweeper boy.

## Word Power

There are several lovely activities in this section. The age and ability of your class will determine your choice.

**Animated Words:** This creative activity allows the children to illustrate words from the story like king, destiny, astrologer, sweeper, etc.

**Big Words:** Big words are so much fun to learn. You can present the children with a few **sesquipedalian words** and ask them how these words relate to the story. Some suggestions would be,

**consequential (kon-si-kwen-shuhl)**
  - following as an effect, as a result of, or outcome

**flabbergast (flab-er-gast)**
  - to overwhelm with shock, surprise or amazement

**gasconade (gas-kuh-neyd)**
  - extravagant boasting or bragging

**hullabaloo (huhl-uh-buh-loo)**
  - a commotion or a fuss

**nincompoop (nin-kuh m-poop)**
  - a foolish or stupid person

**ornery (awr-nuh-ree)**
  • bad tempered or difficult to deal with

**widdershins (with-er-shinz)**
  • counter-clockwise or anti-clockwise, describing the opposite direction from the way a clock moves
  • in the opposite or contrary direction from usual

You can also present the children with some **sesquipedalian phrases** that relate to the story.

It is futile to become lachrymose over precipitately departed lacteal fluids.
(meaning: *Don't cry over spilled milk.*)

Never venture to prognosticate upon the younger generation of poultry until the final process of incubation has been exercised.
(meaning: *Don't count your chickens until they are hatched.*)

If an enclosure for a pedal extremity adapts itself suitably to said appendage, it would be advisable to employ it accordingly.
(meaning: *If the shoe fits, wear it.*)

No individual specimen in the species Homo Sapiens exists in a condition of isolation.
(meaning: *No man is an island.*)


## Name Games

The children can learn the origins and meanings of their names. The activities in this section show the children that names carry attributes and descriptions of identity. Names and their attributes should always reflect the children's very best qualities. The children can know that their name and qualities can change—just as the chimney sweep's name and qualities changed to king of the island country—but the one who knows and watches the changes is the same.

## Mala

The children can use the mala to repeat mantras that gather strength and kingly attitudes such as, *Rām,* or "destiny belongs to the body," or a mantra of their choosing that brings out the nobility in them.

# Timeless Tale 3
# Donkey Riding

There was once a man whose name was Father. Father had a son and a donkey. One day Father decided to travel to the distant village of Dorsta to visit his relations. He thought to take his son and donkey along with him.

Father, along with his son and the donkey, started walking on the road together, setting out on their travels.

Soon they reached the village Pratham, where Father heard some whisperings of criticism from the village folks. He heard them say, "Look at these travellers walking. The young boy looks so tired, why does the father not let his son ride on the donkey?"

Upon hearing this Father became uneasy and immediately placed his son on the donkey while he walked beside them.

In this way, they travelled for some time until they reached the next village, Dosara. As they passed through Dosara, Father heard the whisperings of these village folks saying, "Look at that hard-hearted boy. He is young and healthy, yet he rides on the donkey while his father walks. This is not right."

Upon hearing this criticism Father again became uneasy. In order to deal with the criticism that caused his uneasiness, he told his son to come down from the donkey and he got on in his place.

In this way, they continued on their journey until they reached another village, Teesara. As they passed through this village,

Father heard the whisperings of these village folks saying, "Look at this hard-hearted father. He rides on the donkey and lets his young son walk. This is not right."

Upon hearing this criticism, Father again became uneasy. This time, in order to deal with his uneasiness, Father placed his son on the donkey with him. They both rode on in this way until they reached the next village, called Chautha.

As they passed through Chautha Father heard the whisperings of these village folks saying, "Look at these fools. They are both riding on that poor donkey, who is getting so fatigued and exhausted. Do they not care at all for their donkey?"

Upon hearing this criticism, the father became very upset and uneasy. In order to relieve his uneasiness and show the village folks that he did care for his donkey, Father thought that he and his son should carry the donkey.

Father and his son got some rope and tied the legs of the donkey together. They found a strong pole and placed it between the legs of the donkey. Placing the pole on their shoulders, they hoisted it up and began to carry the donkey. In this way, they travelled until they reached the next village, Panchavan.

When the folks in Panchavan saw this sight—Father and his son carrying their donkey hanging upside down from a pole—they all just laughed out loud and said, "Look at these fools who are carrying their donkey on their shoulders. They certainly do look silly."

After hearing this criticism, Father became so uneasy and uncomfortable that he instructed his son to put the donkey down. Father sat on the grass by the side of the road and thought about the many different comments and criticisms he heard from all the village folks. "Well," he concluded, "There doesn't seem to be anything wrong with any of the village folks, this donkey seems to be the cause of all my uneasiness. I must rid myself of this donkey."

After some deliberation, Father decided to throw the donkey away. He thought this would free him from the criticisms of the village folks and the uneasiness he felt as a result of hearing their words.

Father had his son help him untie the donkey and they started shouting mean and terrible words of criticism at the donkey to scare it away. Then Father and his son continued on their way to visit their relations in the distant village of Dorsta.

*Father was so foolish that he would go to any extent to free himself from criticism and uneasiness. His fear of the loss of his donkey, he could overcome. But his fear of criticism was too hard to drop.*

Now as it happened, a wise man who had also been travelling, had seen all that had happened to Father, his son and the donkey. He watched as they scared the donkey away with their unkind words of criticism.

The wise man befriended the donkey with gentle words of kindness. They became chums, and together the wise man and the donkey rode on to the next village, Chata.

As fate would have it the wise man and the donkey also reached the same village. Immediately Father recognized his donkey, the same donkey that the wise man was riding. Father stopped the wise man and said, "You should not have befriended this donkey and certainly you should not ride it. It will only bring you trouble, criticism and uneasiness.

The wise man looked at Father kindly and said, "There is nothing wrong with this donkey. There was no need for you to have thrown it away. Because you listened to the comments and criticisms of ignorant folks, you threw your intelligence and wit away. You must know that while walking on the path to your goal, you never need to listen to the criticisms of others."

The wise man smiled, waved his hand in farewell, and rode away on the donkey.

# The Lesson
## Donkey Riding

## Theme

The fear of other people's disapproval is a common ailment. In a lighthearted way this story illustrates the uneasiness that takes place when a child or grownup child feels affected by criticism, and the lengths to which he or she will go to be relieved of that uneasiness.

This story is not about judging criticism, the point of the story is how criticism is interpreted and dealt with by the one who is feeling its effects. When children feel small due to criticism, it means that the criticizer and their words have become bigger and more powerful.

Recognizing and pinpointing fear of criticism, is the first step in being released from the capture of its grip. Being armed with the knowledge that fear of criticism exists exclusively in the changing mind, enables children to know that criticism also changes. They can find power and confidence in the freedom and strength of the unchanging Knower.

## Discussion

Introducing relevant vocabulary words and their meanings can help the children pinpoint and express where their shoe pinches. When they know where it pinches, then they can begin to transform their uneasiness into easiness. You can let them know that the sense of easiness always begins with uneasiness.

## Dictionary Meanings

**criticism:**
- the act of saying that something or someone is bad
- the act of giving your opinion or judgement about the good or bad qualities of something or someone

**uneasiness:**
- a feeling of anxiety, worry or discomfort

When having discussions with the children about the effects of criticism, you can remind them of the words the wise man spoke to Father, "There is nothing wrong with this donkey. There was no need for you to have throw it away. Because you listened to the comments and criticisms of ignorant folks, you threw your intelligence and wit away. You must know that while walking on the path to your goal, you never need to listen to the criticisms of others."

## Suggested discussion questions
- What is criticism?
- Have you ever felt like you were criticized?
- How does criticism make you feel?
- Why do you think people criticize others?
- What is uneasiness?
- What did you understand from the story?
- Why do you think the father believed in the words of the village folk?
- What was the silliest thing the father did with the donkey?
- Why do you think people believe in the words of others?

- Are other people's words more powerful in your ears than your own words?
- Do you get affected by criticism when you are asleep? Why not?
- Do you get affected by criticism when you are awake? Why?
- What is the difference between being asleep and being awake?
- Does your mind ever make you feel uneasy?
- Can you pinpoint your mind? Who is doing the pinpointing?
- Where can you go inside yourself to feel the sense of ease?

## Meditation

### Knower Meditation

Meditation on the Knower expands the mind's thinking and concluding mechanism, which will give children fresh perspectives. Placing their attention on the Knower of the thoughts in meditation allows the children to observe and examine words of criticism rather than only react to their effects. You can ask the children to close their eyes and watch as their thoughts come and go like characters on a television screen. The children can ponder over the one who is watching the thoughts and imagine that the watcher has a remote in hand. They can change the criticism channel by placing their attention on the one who is watching. The one who is watching is their own Self, the Knower.

Through meditation and knowledge the children will come to know that they never have to throw their intelligence away. Meditation strengthens the power of the child as watcher, or Knower, and weakens the influence of the thoughts that bind the child to uneasiness. Through continued practice of meditation, the children will come to watch the once powerful words of criticism transform into paper tigers.

## Guided Meditation

You can reread the story while the children close their eyes in meditation and listen. When the story is complete you can ask them to keep their eyes closed and contemplate the words of the wise man, "Because you listened to the comments and criticisms of ignorant folks, you threw your intelligence and wit away. You must know that while walking on the path to your goal, you never need to listen to the criticisms of others."

## Pranayama Meditation

Attending the breath in meditation will focus the minds of the children and bring clarity to their thinking. The children can practice "Awareness of the Movement of Breath" and watch as they attend their natural breath in meditation. They can observe as they breathe in, pause, breathe out, pause, breathe in, pause, breathe out, pause and so forth. This watchfulness empowers the children and can help to safeguard them from the critical words of others. They come to know that all the words are simply sounds that they have given meanings to.

## Mala Meditation

Some children might enjoy using a mala. With every pull of a bead they can breathe—bead one breathe in, bead two pause, bead three breathe out, bead four pause and so forth. For more detailed instructions on the use of the mala please go to "Mala" in the chapter "The Play of Action, Karma Yoga."

# The Play of Breath, Pranayama

Specific instructions on how to perform the breath exercises are found in the chapter "The Play of Breath, Pranayama."

## Humming Bee भ्रमरी प्राणायाम Bhramarī Prāṇāyām

The children can scare away the words of criticism with the sound of the Humming Bee.

## Alternate Nostril Breathing
## अनुलोम-विलोम प्राणायाम Anulom-Vilom Prāṇāyām

The children can breathe in easiness and breathe out criticism in this alternating breath exercise.

## Bellows Breath भस्त्रिका प्राणायाम Bhastrikā Prāṇāyām

With the breath of a bellows, the children can blow away the village folks' words of criticism. This exercise brings about the sense of balance and ease.

## Abdominal Breathing अधम प्राणायाम Adham Prāṇāyām

This full breath builds strength in the children's system while it calms and stabilizes their disposition. Then, like the wise man, they never have to listen to the criticisms of others.

## The Sound of Om प्रणव प्राणायाम Pranav Prāṇāyām

This pranayama is fantastic for bringing focus, peace and steadiness to the mind. As the children watch the natural inclination of their own breathing pattern, they can fill each breath with either the sound of *Om*, the word "peace" or any mantra that soothes their minds and fills them with peace and ease.

## King of Pranayama
## केवल कुम्भक प्राणायाम Keval Kumbhak Prāṇāyām

Holding and attending the space between each breath is where neither criticism, uneasiness or even easiness can reach. It is the state of perfect stillness, the Knower state.

# The Play of Sound, Mantra

Information and specific instructions on pronunciation of mantras are found in the chapter "The Play of Sound, Mantra."

## Shyām श्याम

The mantra *Shyām* characterizes the space that is untouched by criticism. This must have been the mantra that the wise man repeated *ShyāmaShyāmaShyāmaShyām...*

## Hum हं

The sound *Hum* creates ease and comfort. When repeating this mantra, the sense of criticism will expand the individual sense of "I" to the universal sense of "I" which means "I as That." When repeating this mantra the sense of criticism will melt away.

## So Hum सो हं

With this mantra the children can transform the sense of uneasiness into the sense of easiness just by using their breath.

## Om Shānti ॐ शान्ति

The resonance of the sound of the mantra *Om Shānti* invokes peaceful tranquility. It is a great mantra to transform a space of unease to one of ease. *Om Shānti Shānti Shānti*

## Mantras of your own choosing

It can be fascinating to discuss with the children what sounds, words, meanings and languages would help soothe them when they feel the effects of criticism, for example, "Believe in your Self, Believe in your Knower."

# The Play of Body, Hatha Yoga

Specific instructions on how to perform the poses can be found in the chapter "The Play of Body, Hatha Yoga."

## Mountain Pose ताडासन Tādāsan

The children can stand tall and firm while remembering the words of the wise man. "You must know that while walking on the path to your goal, you never need to listen to the criticisms of others."

## Cobra Pose भुजङ्गासन Bhujangāsan

As the children hold this pose, they can hiss at the words of criticism to scare them away.

## Bridge Pose सेतुबन्धसर्वाङ्गासन Setu Bandh Sarvāngāsan

The children can cross the bridge of criticism and uneasiness to strength, wisdom and ease, knowing that all feelings and responses will change. The one who watches them change, never changes.

## Lion Pose सिंघासन Singhāsan

While performing this pose, the children can scare away unwanted thoughts and feelings that make them feel bad about themselves. They can imbibe the majestic qualities of the king of the jungle.

## Warrior Poses वीरभद्रासन Vīrabhadrāsan

In these warrior poses the children can pretend to aim and shoot their arrows, or draw their swords, at the words of criticism that are trying to harm them. They can imbibe the skill and strength of a warrior who can shoot down the thoughts and criticisms that aim to hurt.

## Corpse Pose or Immortal Pose शवासन Shavāsan

If a child feels the effects of criticism, it is always great for her or him to take a break, rest and rejuvenate the body and mind. This subtle pose allows the child to be with the eternal sense of their own Self, the Knower.

# The Play of Action, Karma Yoga

The instructions for these activities can be found in the chapter "The Play of Action, Karma Yoga."

## Retell the Story

You can ask the children if they can recall the criticisms of the different village folks in order of occurrence.

You can have fun playing a call and response game. Divide the class into two groups. The first group can be the group called "Call" and the second called "Response." The "Call" group starts first, they will try as a group to recall, in order of occurrence, the way in which Father, his son and the donkey walked to each village. The "Response" group will recall the criticism of the folks from that village. Each group of children should try to speak in unison. This activity can be a lot of fun.

## Doctor's Diagnosis

The children can take on the roles of patient and doctor trying to cure abstract ailments. Patient Registration and Doctor's Diagnosis forms are provided.

The role of the patient would be a character from the story. For example, Father can be seeking a cure for uneasiness due to hearing criticisms. The donkey can be seeking a cure for dealing with feelings of being blamed for something it didn't do. A village folk could be looking for a cure to stop criticizing others.

The role of the doctor would be to investigate and question the patient about his or her symptoms. The doctor will consult with the patient, diagnose his or her condition and prescribe a cure. Playing both roles is a great way for children to examine, pinpoint and express where their shoe pinches.

You can make adjustments to this activity to meet the age and ability of your students.

## Broken Telephone

Broken telephone is a lot of fun to play with a group of children. It demonstrates the cumulative errors and inaccuracies that can occur between a speaker and a listener—between what is spoken and what is heard. Sometimes a person may hear a compliment as a criticism and vise versa. This lively activity demonstrates how words that are spoken and repeated over and over again, take on a life of their own.

## Word Power

There are a number of activities where the children become aware of the power behind the spoken word. As seen in this story the spoken word led Father to such uneasiness that he threw his own donkey away. The activities in this section will give the children a chance to play with words, discover their power and even animate them.

### Sesquipedalian Words

You can present some sesquipedalian words and ask the children how they relate to the story.

**befuddle (bih-fuhd-l)**
- unable to think clearly
- to confuse, perplex, bewilder, baffle or muddle

**bombastic (bom-bas-tik)**
- saying something important sounding with no real meaning
- pompous, grandiose, pretentious

**consequential (kon-si-kwen-shuhl)**
- following as an effect, as a result of, or outcome

**disadvantageous (dis-ad-vuh n-tey-juhs)**
- creating unfavourable circumstances that reduce the chances of success or effectiveness

**discombobulate (dis-kuhm-bob-yuh-leyt)**
- to confuse someone or make someone feel uncomfortable

**flabbergast (flab-er-gast)**
- to overwhelm with shock, surprise or amazement

**idiosyncrasy (id-ee-oh-sin-kruh-see)**
- a characteristic, mode of behaviour or way of thought that is peculiar to an individual

**nincompoop (nin-kuh m-poop)**
- a foolish or stupid person

**Sesquipedalian phrases**

Individuals who make their abode in vitreous edifices would be advised to refrain from catapulting projectiles.
(meaning: People who live in glass houses shouldn't throw stones.)

Missiles of ligneous or petrous consistency have the potential of fracturing my osseous structure, but appellations will remain sempiternally innocuous.
(meaning: Sticks and stones can break my bones, but names will never hurt me.)

A complete selection is provided in "The Play of Action, Karma Yoga" under the heading "Word Power."

## Mirror Breath

Children can look at themselves in the clear mirror. Then they can fog it up with their breath. Using their finger on the foggy mirror, they can write or draw how they felt when they were criticized. When they finish expressing all that they need to, you can suggest that they wipe the mirror clean and ask where their feelings have gone.

## Timeline

This activity helps develop linear thinking as the children use their memory to recall the story's events. You can have them use the provided Timeline or Comic Strip.

The children can create a visual representation of the village folks criticisms and Father's uneasy response to each one. As the story builds we watch the level of uneasiness in Father grow with every criticism. Father believed in, and reacted to, the criticisms with increased uneasiness and loss of perspective. It can be interesting for children to observe that through repeated criticism, uneasiness builds. It is a cycle that doesn't have to happen.

## Grumpy T-Shirt

If a child is feeling uneasy because of criticism, sometimes he or she should just make a Grumpy T-Shirt about it.

# Timeless Tale 4
# Fox and Camel

*There are some friends who always play tricks, take advantage and insist there is nothing wrong with their actions. They maintain that the problem belongs to you alone. Sometimes your brain should work for you.*

It happened once that a fox named Fox, and a camel named Camel, became friends, because in the forest nobody else was there. Fox had no friends and Camel had no friends. Sometimes such friendships happen. When there is no one else around, then whoever is there becomes your friend.

Early one morning Camel said to his friend, "I am very hungry, there is nothing for me to eat in this forest. You are a little fox and can eat a small amount and be satisfied, but what can I do?"

Now, Fox desired to have a ride on Camel's back and she was smart enough to know how to get what she wanted. Fox said, "I will take you to a wonderful garden where there are many good things for you to eat, but it is quite far away. Perhaps you can let me ride on your back."

"Certainly," said Camel. "I don't mind because I am very hungry. Hop on and let us be on our way."

In order for Fox to get a good ride on Camel's back, she started to order him about, telling him first to go here and then to go there. Fox was very much enjoying her ride.

They came to a river bank and Fox told her friend that a farmer's garden, with many delicious things to eat, lay across this river. So with Fox on Camel's back the two of them crossed the river. They wandered about until they came to the farmer's garden.

In the garden they saw lots of cucumbers, melons and pumpkins. Fox asked her friend to let her get down so she could eat and roam about. Camel replied, "No, no, no, Fox. You must let me eat first."

"Why?" asked Fox. "I said I would bring you to a garden and here it is. Now you say that you want to be selfish and you won't let me come down to eat."

"Look Fox," said Camel, "You are smarter than me and you have a very small stomach. If I let you down, you will play a trick on me. You will eat and run away. Then I will be left alone feeling very insecure. I do not know my way around and something bad may happen to me. So I don't want to let you down just yet."

Fox replied to her friend, "I cannot run far away because of the river, and the river I cannot cross unless you take me on your back. So you should not feel insecure. You must believe in me Camel, I am your friend."

In the name of friendship Camel was convinced and decided to trust his friend. He let Fox down and she ran all about. She ran here and there, she hopped about nibbling on this and munching on that. When she was finished eating she said to her friend, "My dear Camel, I have eaten my fill and I feel very satisfied. I now have an urge to sing."

*Now the design of Camel is that once he drinks and eats, it is enough for several days. But Camel has such a big stomach that it takes time for him to eat and drink. He cannot be satisfied with just a few cucumbers.*

So Camel said to his friend, "No, no, Fox, please. I have not even half-finished eating. Please do not sing at this time. Do not play this trick on me. If you do you will surely wake up the farmer who must still be sleeping."

"But I have an urge," Fox insisted, "It is my preference. I always sing after I eat."

"Please Fox, don't do it," Camel pleaded. "You are really going to invite trouble for me."

"I cannot resist this urge. I have feelings to express. I really must sing. It is the habit pattern of a fox." And Fox began to sing her morning song.

Well, the farmer was awakened by the song of Fox and he immediately rushed to check on his garden. Fox spotted the farmer coming, and being a very agile and smart little creature, she quickly ran away leaving Camel alone in the cucumber patch.

When the farmer arrived, he found Camel in his garden eating his cucumbers. You can well imagine that Camel's appetite is not for one cucumber. Camel ate almost all the cucumbers in the garden. Upon seeing this, the farmer became very angry and took a stick and began to beat Camel. Camel started to run away but he was not very fast.

Because of the loss of a few cucumbers and his feelings of anger, the farmer took his revenge on Camel. The poor fellow was beaten a lot as the farmer chased him away.

Camel ran and ran until finally he reached the bank of the river. Out of friendship he stood around waiting for Fox to show up.

Meanwhile, Fox had eaten a second and third meal and was just loitering about. When Fox and Camel finally met up with each other, Fox asked, "How did you fare?"

"Not very well," answered Camel, "I was beaten by the farmer."

"Why?" asked Fox.

"Because the farmer came and caught me eating his cucumbers," Camel said.

"Why did he come?" asked Fox. "It was very early in the morning."

"He came because he heard you singing your morning song and it woke him up," Camel announced.

"Well, I was not singing knowingly," Fox replied, "It was out of my urge that I sang."

"Well, your urge caused my beating. Did you not understand what your urge would do to me?" Camel retorted.

Fox said nothing.

Camel sat quietly to ponder and reflect on what he understood.

Camel remembered that Fox ran away and left him alone in the cucumber patch where the farmer found him and beat him. He understood that he was beaten because of Fox and her urge to sing—even when he asked her not to. He understood that the farmer woke up because he heard Fox singing her morning song.

*Camel understood that Fox was smart enough to bring him to a place where she knew she could escape when she sensed trouble.*

After much deliberation, Camel decided to plan his revenge.

Fox sat quietly waiting for Camel to say something. Finally she said, "Well, what are we waiting for? Let us proceed to our abode. Let me climb on your back and we can go across the river."

"Fine," said Camel, and he bent down to let Fox climb on his back.

With Fox on his back, Camel started to cross the river. When they reached the middle, where the water was up to Camel's stomach, he said to his friend, "My dear friend Fox, I have an urge."

Fox said, "What urge do you have? Do you want to go back and eat cucumbers? You have already been beaten."

"No, no, not that urge," he said, "I have an urge to take a bath."

"You have an urge to take a bath?" Fox questioned, "What kind of a trick are you playing on me?"

Camel said, "No, no, I really have an urge to take a bath. I want to wash my stomach and my back, my hump and my head and my ears. I really must have a bath."

"Well, your neck is long enough. You can dip it into the water and your ears, eyes and lips will be cleaned," Fox assured him.

"I want to wash my hump but it is too far away from my mouth," Camel said. "I must wash my hump because you are sitting on it and you made it very dirty."

"Please don't do this," Fox implored. "If you take a bath now I will be thrown into the river. You do not realize how fast this current is. My legs are very short and I will not be able to easily swim in it."

"But I really have an urge to take a bath," Camel insisted.

"Please, Camel. Please don't do this," Fox begged.

*Fox was always playing tricks on Camel, but now she did not have one trick more. No trick came to her mind or heart at that time and she could not please her friend. Fox could not think of anything more to say; rather, she continued to boss him around. Camel was getting angrier and angrier. He remembered the farmer's beating because of the trick that Fox had played on him.*

Then, Camel just relaxed and leaned back, and Fox was thrown from Camel's back and had to cross the river herself.

After taking his revenge, Camel waded to the shore.

*So sometimes it happens that the tricks of Fox do not work, and the tricks of Camel do. In order to survive in the world, Camel must know some kind of knowledge about how to take care of himself and how to deal with friends like Fox, who try to take advantage and make fools of him.*

*Your brain should work under all circumstances.*

# The Lesson
## Fox and Camel

### Theme

This charming tale meanders through the adventures of two friends, Fox and Camel, who have very different personalities. Fox is always playing tricks, taking advantage and getting Camel into trouble. Camel is slow-moving and likes to go along with his friend...until one day Camel decides enough is enough.

**It is important to note** that this story is an allegory and does not advocate throwing a friend into the river as Camel did to Fox.

Fox represents the kinds of thoughts and ideas that get children into trouble. It is such thoughts that can be thrown from the minds of children—just as Fox was thrown from Camel's back.

Camel represents the one who knows but doesn't act on his inner knowing. Camel knew that he was going to be beaten by the farmer if Fox sang her morning song, and he still remained in the cucumber patch unable to prevent the inevitable.

Children may relate to the personalities and situations of Fox and Camel. They can be reminded that personalities and situations change, but the one who knows and watches them does not change. The one who knows and watches, is their own unchanging Self, the Knower.

Through this story the children can learn to reclaim the knowledge and dignity of their own inner wisdom. They can learn to trust in their own inner knowledge, the Knower. Then they will have the executive ability to deal with situations that come their way.

## Discussion

You can talk to the children about friendship—how they make friends, what they like about their friends and what their friendships are based on. Sometimes friends are people who are there, as was the case with Fox and Camel.

This timeless tale showcases the friendship of two very different personalities who are friends because of circumstances. Fox has a fun-loving nature and easily takes advantage of others in order to get what she wants. Camel likes to go along with his friend's ideas, he doesn't listen to his inner wisdom, even when he knows better.

At the end of the story, Camel reclaims his strength and dignity by deciding to throw his bondage, in the form of Fox, into the river.

## Dictionary Meanings

**friend:**
- a person who you know well and like a lot, but who is usually not a member of your family

**friendship:**
- a relationship between friends

**fox:**
- a carnivorous mammal of the Canidae or dog family with a pointed muzzle and bushy tail
- (personified) a cunning or crafty person.

**camel:**
- A camel is a large long-necked hoofed mammal that lives in desert regions. They have long legs and broad cushioned feet that help them walk in the sand. They have big-lipped snouts, nostrils that can open and close and long eyelashes to protect them from blowing sand. Camels have either one hump or two; a camel with one hump is called a Dromedary and a camel with two humps is called a Bactrian. When food and water is available, camels eat and drink in large amounts and store the food and water as fat in their hump. That is why they are able to survive in the desert for long periods without eating or drinking. They are domestic animals used for carrying goods and people.
- (personified) a slow moving, obedient and obstinate person

**revenge:**
- the action of harming someone in return for a wrong suffered at their hands
- an act of retaliating in order to get even

Meditation is a great technique that allows the children to pause and get in touch with the Knower inside. By taking a pause, they will gain the strength and discrimination to throw away the thoughts that blind and bind them to unpleasant consequences. Then they will have the space and openness to allow fresh new perspectives to enter their minds. Power is in the "pause." The "pause" is like a reset button.

## Colloquial Expressions

**The straw that broke the camel's back.**
It refers to loading up a camel beyond its capacity where the weight of one final piece of straw becomes the cause of the camel's collapse. The small, seemingly insignificant addition to a burden renders it too much to bear.

## Suggested Discussion Questions

- What is a friend?
- How do you make friends?
- What is friendship?
- What does it mean to be a friend?
- What do you expect from a friend?
- Have you ever felt like you were taken advantage of by a friend?
- Have you ever felt pressure to do something you didn't want to do? If so, how did you deal with it?
- What do you think the story is really about?
- How do you deal with thoughts in your mind that make you feel bad?
- What happens to your friends when you are asleep?
- Where is your mind when you are asleep?
- Can you think of ways to take a "pause" to reset or refresh your thoughts and outlook?
- Can you think of ways to make yourself feel better?
- Who watches the things that happen to you?

# Meditation

## Pranayama Meditation

Meditation on the breath calms the fidgety, agitated mind that feels the pressure of other people's expectations. The movement of breath is directly linked to the movement of the mind. When children feel pressure they can pause and hold their breath for a moment to centre themselves. This meditation is wonderful for creating a sense of ease and balance in their nervous system. The children can use the breath exercise "Awareness of the Movement of Breath" in this meditation. You can ask them to focus their awareness on the movement of their breath. Ask them to pay attention on the friends in the story; they can inhale to Fox and pause, exhale to Camel and pause, inhale to Fox and pause, exhale to Camel and pause, etc. In this way, Fox and Camel become friends as both are integrally part of the movement of breath. After a few rounds of watching the movement of breath, their minds will feel refreshed.

## Guided Meditation

You can talk about friends and friendships with the children and then ask them to close their eyes and sit comfortably as you reread the story.

## Knower Meditation

Ask the children to watch as their thoughts come into their minds, stay for some time and then dissolve making way for new thoughts to arise. You can then ask the children to place their attention on the one who is watching the changing thoughts that come and go and change. The one watching the changes of the mind is not changing. The one watching is their own Self, the Knower. Through placing their attention on the Knower in meditation, the children come to see that the mind, thoughts and personality are always changing, but the one watching and knowing the changes is always there. By aligning themselves with the peace and strength of the unchanging Knower, they will always find a way to take care of themselves.

# The Play of Breath, Pranayama

Specific instructions on how to perform the breath exercises are found in the chapter "The Play of Breath, Pranayama."

## Chanting Breath उद्गीथ प्राणायाम Udgīth Prānāyām

This breath exercise involves chanting. The children can chant a morning song like Fox liked to do. When chanting the sweet, peaceful mantra *Om* or *Hum*, the farmer would most likely, stay home, rather than run to the cucumber patch to beat Camel. He would stay at home to meditate on the melodious sound of the children's morning song.

## Shining Forehead
## कपालभाति प्राणायाम Kapālbhāti Prānāyām

This exercise can energize and uplift the mind of a child who might feel burdened by the antics of a friend. The child will gain strength in her or his understanding as their mind begins to work clearly through practicing this exercise.

## Cooling Breath शीतली प्राणायाम Shītalī Prānāyām

When children are feeling hot under the collar, this cooling breath will calm their minds and cool their feelings of anger. This breathing exercise involves sticking out their tongues and curling them like straws. As the children inhale through their curled tongues, they can watch as the heat of their anger transforms into the cooling calm of their own breath. And sticking out their tongues to anger, is a bonus.

For children who have difficulty curling their tongues, they can make a small "O" shape with their lips instead. For more detailed instructions please check Cooling Breath in "The Play of Breath, Pranayama."

## Balanced Breathing
## सम-वृत्ति प्राणायाम Sam-Vritti Prānāyām

This exercise brings balance to the children's minds and nervous systems. You can ask them to visualize a square with Fox sitting on top of it. They can inhale to the count of two and then pause to the count of two. Then they can visualize Camel underneath with the box on his hump as they exhale to the count of two and then pause to the count of two. Please note that holding the exhalation is more difficult than holding the inhalation. As they complete a few rounds, they can watch as Fox and Camel become friends and their breathing becomes a breath of fresh air.

## Alternate Nostril Breathing
## अनुलोम-विलोम प्राणायाम Anulom-Vilom Prānāyām

This breath exercise is like the two unlikely friends, Fox and Camel, who are opposite to each other—*anulom* means "to go with the grain" and *vilom* means "to go against the grain." While performing this alternate nostril breathing exercise, the children can alternate between Fox and Camel, knowing that it is not about two friends or two nostrils. It is one nose with two nostrils, and one breath with two functions (inhalation and exhalation). The breath is one and the same in all beings.

## Victory Breath or Ocean Breath
## उज्जायी प्राणायाम Ujjayī Prānāyām

The real victory is when there is clarity of mind and the brain works properly. When the children's thoughts and ideas get them into trouble, it is time to throw those thoughts and ideas in the ocean. This is the breath of victory.

## The Play of Sound, Mantra

Information and specific instructions on pronunciation of mantras are found in the chapter "The Play of Sound, Mantra."

## Amaram Hum Madhuram Hum अमरम् हं मधुरम् हं

This very special mantra brings the attention to the Knower state of consciousness. It focuses the awareness on the one who is watching Fox and Camel play their tricks on each other. They know all the while that tricks will change, but the one who watches them will remain forever peaceful and free. The one who watches is their own Self, the Knower.

## Jai Rām Shrī Rām जय राम श्री राम

This mantra carries perfection and virtue in its resonance. The children can make up their own tune to this very lovely mantra that celebrates the victory of the unchanging Knower over the changing tricks of Fox and Camel.
*Jai Rām Shrī Rām Jai Jai Rām,*
*Jai Rām Shrī Rām Jai Jai Rām.*

## Hare Krishna Hare Rām हरे कृष्ण हरे राम

The children can be like Fox who always had an urge to sing. They can chant this lovely mantra that made its way into popular culture through George Harrison who included this mantra in the song he wrote called "My Sweet Lord." This lovely mantra can be sung with that tune.

## Om ॐ

This universal mantra can be the children's morning song. When they sing *Om* they are echoing the sound and meaning of universal peace.

## Om Shānti ॐ शान्ति

This resounding sound of peace can give the children the opportunity to create some lovely tunes with this simple and elegant mantra. *Om Shānti Shānti Shānti*

## Hum हं

Through this mantra, the children will come to know that the friends Fox and Camel, will change and their tricks will change, but the "I" or *Hum* who is watching the changes is ever the same and unchanging, the Knower of who they are.

## Mantras of your own choosing

The children can have fun creating mantras that relate to their own sense of freedom, peace and humour. Selecting mantras from different languages can also be fun.

# The Play of Body, Hatha Yoga

Specific instructions on how to perform the poses can be found in the chapter "The Play of Body, Hatha Yoga."

This story is about friendships. It can be fun for the children to practice the poses in pairs or in groups.

## Downward-Facing Dog Pose
## अधोमुखश्वानासन Adho Mukh Shwānāsan

This pose relates to both Fox and Camel. A fox is classified as part of the Canidae or dog family, while performing this pose, the children can pretend to be Fox. The children can also pretend to be Camel because when held, this pose resembles the hump on Camel's back. Have fun with this dual-purpose pose.

## Forward-Fold Pose उत्तानासन Uttānāsan

When the children bend their body forward in this pose, they resemble Camel with a very high hump. They will look like Camel after he has eaten his fill of cucumbers.

## Cat Poses मार्जरीआसन/बिडालासन Mārjārīāsan/Bidālāsan

The children can have fun with this two-step pose. When they perform *mārjārīāsan* their backs will round out like the hump on Camel's back. When they perform *bidālāsan*, their backs will arch inward and resemble Fox. This pose demonstrates that in one pose, both friends can transform into one another. The one performing the pose is the source of both.

## Boat Poses नावासन Nāvāsan

These boat poses are for those children who don't have a camel at their disposal when they would like to cross a river. This is a fun pose for the children to perform in pairs as they hold the boat poses together and cross the river to the other side.

## Sphinx Pose सलम्ब भुजङ्गासन Salamb Bhujangāsan

Children can always use a little support from a friend. *Salamb* means support. The children can support their backs with their arms as they hold this pose.

## Bridge Pose सेतुबन्धसर्वाङ्गासन Setu Bandh Sarvāngāsan

Sometimes the children can use a bridge to cross the river. Sometimes a bridge is needed for joining friends together. And sometimes this pose looks like a camel's hump. This pose can be done in pairs or groups.

## Sun Salutation Poses
## सूर्यनमस्कारासन Sūrya Namaskārāsan

This is a lovely series of poses that friends can do in unison.

You can also have the children make their own series of poses to tell the story of Fox and Camel.

# The Play of Action, Karma Yoga

The instructions for these activities can be found in the chapter "The Play of Action, Karma Yoga."

## Complaint Report

This activity provides the children with an opportunity to isolate an event and point of view. In this way, through filling out a complaint report they get to walk in someone else's shoes. The children can fill out the provided Complaint Report from the point of view of different characters in the story. For example, the farmer could complain about Fox waking him up, and about Camel who he found in his cucumber patch eating all his cucumbers. Camel could fill out a complaint report about Fox who left him alone in the cucumber patch, and about the farmer who beat him just for eating his cucumbers. Fox could fill out a complaint report about Camel having an urge to take a bath.

## Building Bridges

This activity requires group cooperation, problem solving and expression, in order for the group to make the bridge and complete the activity. Sometimes friends need to learn how to figure things out with each other.

## Word Power

Children can find power in the words they use. They can **animate words** from the story and they can also learn some **big words**. Here are some **sesquipedalian words** that suit this story.

**anthropomorphism (an-thruh-puh-mawr-fiz-uhm)**
- the attribution of human characteristics or behaviours to an animal or object

**befuddle (bih-fuhd-l)**
- unable to think clearly
- to confuse, perplex, bewilder, baffle or muddle

**bombastic (bom-bas-tik)**
- saying something important sounding with no real meaning
- pompous, grandiose, pretentious

**consequential (kon-si-kwen-shuhl)**
- following as an effect, as a result of, or outcome

**disadvantageous (dis-ad-vuh n-tey-juhs)**
- creating unfavourable circumstances that reduce the chances of success or effectiveness

**discombobulate (dis-kuhm-bob-yuh-leyt)**
- to confuse someone or make someone feel uncomfortable

**extemporaneous (eks-tem-puh-rey-nee-uhs)**
- spoken or done without preparation
- uttered on the spur of the moment

**hullabaloo (huhl-uh-buh-loo)**
- a commotion or a fuss

**idiosyncrasy (id-ee-oh-sin-kruh-see)**
- a characteristic, mode of behaviour or way of thought that is peculiar to an individual

**nincompoop (nin-kuh m-poop)**
- a foolish or stupid person

Suggested **sesquipedalian phrases**.

It is futile to become lachrymose over precipitately departed lacteal fluids. (meaning: *Don't cry over spilled milk.*)

Missiles of ligneous or petrous consistency have the potential of fracturing my osseous structure, but appellations will remain sempiternally innocuous.
(meaning: *Sticks and stones can break my bones, but names will never hurt me.*)

The person presenting the ultimate cachinnation possesses thereby the optimal cachinnation.
(meaning: *He who laughs last, laughs best.*)


## Back-to-Back Communication

Like Fox and Camel, the children can learn to talk and listen to each other through this communication activity that requires them to both speak and listen to each other.

## Grumpy T-Shirt

Sometimes children just want to express their grumpiness. They can do so in this activity.

## Timeline

The children can document the story's events sequentially on the provided Timeline or Comic Strip. Depending on their age and ability, the children can either draw the events or write them in. They can also create their own comic strip adventures.

## Mirrors

The children can have fun mirroring the actions of their friends. One child can be the one looking in the mirror while the other child is the reflection. They can have fun practicing hatha yoga poses as well as performing pranks that will be mirrored back to them by their friends.

# Timeless Tale 5
## Kalpataru

*There is a magical tree called Kalpataru. It has the power to manifest whatever you think of or whatever you wish for. If you ever find yourself sitting under that tree, then whatever your thoughts or wishes may be, that will happen. That will all come to pass.*

As the story goes, there was once a boy who took a long walk in the forest. When he was quite fatigued and exhausted from his walk, he sat down under the shade of a tree to take rest. He did not know that he sat down under the magical *Kalpataru* tree. He did not know that while sitting under this tree all his thoughts and wishes were going to come true.

As he leaned against the tree he thought to himself, "What very lovely shade there is under this tree."

Immediately, all around him the shade came.

He thought, "This is so nice. It almost feels as if it will begin to drizzle soon."

It started to drizzle.

Then he thought, "Oh, it is very nice here, everything is so fine. But it is beginning to feel a little cool now. I wish there was some sun to warm me."

At once the sun appeared and warmed him.

"Hmmm," he thought. "I am a little hungry. I wish I had some food."

Just then a basket filled with delicious food appeared.

He was a little surprised to see this, but as he was very hungry he just started to eat.

He began to wonder how all this was happening. He didn't know that he was sitting under the *Kalpataru* tree. He didn't know that everything that was happening was the outcome of his own thought.

After eating his fill, he sat quietly under the tree feeling very satisfied. He then started to think that he was feeling a little lonely and would like some company.

At that very moment some lovely friends manifested right before his eyes.

"Well," he thought to himself, "Now that these lovely friends have come, there should also be some nice toys for us to play with."

Immediately some fabulous toys appeared, and he and his friends began to play.

They played for some time and then he became tired. He wondered when his friends were going to go home.

His friends disappeared.

While sitting under the *Kalpataru* tree he thought about many things. In their turn, everything he thought about came into manifestation right before his eyes. Whatever he thought about, whatever he wished for, all that came to him.

As he sat pondering under the tree, he thought, "Well, I'm actually all alone here in this forest."

As soon as he had this thought, everything disappeared and he was all alone.

He looked around and started to think, "I wonder if there are any lions in this part of the forest."

Just then a lion appeared.

Upon seeing the lion, he became frightened and thought, "Will the lion notice me?"

The lion came nearer.

"Oh my," he thought. "I wonder if this lion will eat me."

And the lion ate him.

*That is the power of the magical Kalpataru tree. If you ever find yourself sitting under that tree, then you will have to be very, very careful. Because whatever you think of, or whatever you wish for, that will surely come to pass.*

# The Lesson

## Kalpataru

## Theme

This amusing little tale is the perfect platform to have fun and explore the power of the mind—its changeable nature and all the adventures and exciting places it can take both children and grown-up children. The mind, with its power to manifest thoughts, wishes and desires, can be likened to the *Kalpataru* tree. Whatever the mind thinks of or wishes for, people make efforts and work to get what they want.

It is important to try to place the attention on the one who watches the changeable nature of the mind with all its escapades. The one who watches is you, and goes by the name Knower.

## Discussion

> The Lorax: Which way does a tree fall?
> The Once-ler: Uh, down?
> The Lorax: A tree falls the way it leans. Be careful which way
> you lean. (Dr Seuss, 1971, *The Lorax*)

Thoughts are powerful. They colour and shape how children view their world. When children have happy thoughts, their outlook is happy. When they have gloomy thoughts, their outlook is gloomy. Children differ from one another and should have the opportunity to explore their own thoughts and inclinations—

what makes them happy and unhappy, what makes them easy and uneasy, and what are their likes and dislikes. By exploring their own uniqueness, children discover the similarities and differences with one another. Through observation, they come to see what makes each of them tick.

This story provides a great opportunity to examine how to make choices and how to decide what to wish for. Understanding their minds, inclinations and preferences helps the children determine what their choices and wishes are based on.

## Dictionary Meanings

Presenting dictionary meanings of pertinent words helps the children articulate their thoughts and feelings about the story.

**wish:**
- an expression of a desire, typically in the form of a request

**thought:**
- an idea or opinion produced by thinking, occurring in the mind

**choice:**
- an act of deciding between two or more possibilities

**consequence:**
- a result or effect of an action or situation, typically one that is unwelcome or unpleasant

## Colloquial Expressions:

The expressions below can be fun to discuss and explore with the children.

**If you lie down with dogs, you'll wake up with fleas.**
It means, be cautious of the company you keep. If you associate with bad people, you'll acquire their habits.

**The proof is in the pudding.**
It means that you can only judge something after you have tried it.

**Be careful what you wish for; it just might come true.**
It means that you may get what you wish for, but there may be unforeseen, even unpleasant consequences attached to your wish.

This story illustrates that if you aren't careful with your thoughts and wishes, they might eat you up.

> In this world there are only two tragedies. One is not getting what one wants, and the other is getting it. The last is much the worst; the last is a real tragedy!
> (Oscar Wilde, 1893, *Lady Windermere's Fan*, Act 3)

## Suggested Discussion Questions

- If you were granted three wishes, what would they be?
- From the story, can you remember the thoughts and wishes in order? What thought was first, second, etc.?
- What was the last thought the boy had?
- What does "consequences" mean?
- How are choices made?
- What are your likes and dislikes?
- Are your likes and dislikes the same as your friends?
- Why do you think people have different likes and dislikes, and different thoughts and wishes?
- Who chooses your thoughts and wishes?
- How do you choose?
- How do you know what suits you and what does not?
- Where do thoughts come from?

- If you had a dream about the *Kalpataru* tree, where would your dream thoughts be when you wake up?
- Where do your thoughts go when you are asleep?
- Are you the same person when you are asleep, as you are when you are awake? How do you know?
- Who watches the changing thoughts?
- Is there something that always remains the same, unchanging and knowing?
- What is unique about you?

# Meditation

## Guided Meditation

Have the children sit in meditation and imagine that they are sitting under the *Kalpataru* tree while you reread the story to them.

You can guide the children's meditation by asking them to contemplate where thoughts come from and where thoughts go to. You can lead their attention to who is watching the thoughts come, stay for some time and then dissolve back from where they came. You can let them know that the one who is watching is their own Self, the Knower.

## Knower Meditation

You can lead the children into meditation by asking them to think about where their thoughts and desires come from.

Ask them to place their attention on who is watching and knowing the thoughts. The one knowing and watching is their own Self, the Knower. The Knower is there before the thoughts arrive and after they depart. The Knower is there when their thoughts are present and when they are not. You can let them know that the

Knower state of consciousness is like a movie screen on which all their thoughts are projected.

Through meditation on the Knower, the children's minds become absorbed in its unchanging space of peace and delight. As a result, a sense of clarity begins to appear in their mind. With this clarity the children develop the power and strength to make decisions that work for their own well-being.

## The Play of Breath, Pranayama

Specific instructions on how to perform the breath exercises are found in the chapter "The Play of Breath, Pranayama."

## Awareness of the Movement of Breath
## प्राण चिन्तन प्राणायाम Prān Chintan Prānāyām

The movement of breath is linked to the movement of mind. While performing this exercise, the children should pay careful attention to the thoughts and wishes entering their minds, staying for a while and then departing. They can contemplate who is watching the changes. The one watching the changes is their own Self, the Knower.

## Chanting Breath उद्गीथ प्राणायाम Udgīth Prānāyām

The children can chant or whisper their wishes on the exhalation of this chanting breath. Ask them to place their attention on their inner most thoughts and wishes.

## Cooling Breath शीतली प्राणायाम Shītalī Prānāyām

When the boy first sat under the *Kalpataru* tree, he wanted to rest and cool off after his long walk. The children can cool themselves off with this cooling breath. As they inhale through their straw-shaped tongues, they can try to listen for the rustle of leaves coming from the *Kalpataru* tree.

For children who have difficulty curling their tongues, they can make a small "O" shape with their lips instead. For more detailed instructions please check Cooling Breath in "The Play of Breath, Pranayama."

## Warming Breath सूर्य भेदि प्राणायाम Sūrya Bhedi Prānāyām

The children can be reminded of the boy who was sitting under the *Kalpataru* tree and became a little chilly after it had drizzled. He thought to have the sun come out and warm him. This breath will warm the children as the sun warmed the boy.

## Abdominal Breathing अधम प्राणायाम Adham Prānāyām

The children can observe how thoughts and wishes may differ according to different breathing techniques. With the full breath of this exercise, perhaps their wishes will come true.

## Bellows Breath भस्त्रिका प्राणायाम Bhastrikā Prānāyām

The children can breathe in and breath out like a bellows creating a current of air that fans a fire. They can do this very gently, slowly and evenly as they observe their thoughts and wishes dance before them and disappear like fire sparks that fly out of the flames.

# The Play of Sound, Mantra

Information and specific instructions on pronunciation of mantras are found in the chapter "The Play of Sound, Mantra."

## Amaram Hum Madhuram Hum अमरम् हं मधुरम् हं

The magic of this mantra matches the magic of the *Kalpataru* tree. The *Kalpataru* tree fulfills the thoughts and wishes of the mind while the mantra *Amaram Hum Madhuram Hum* fulfills the wish to know the Knower.

## So Hum सो हं

This mantra is a reflection of the sound of breath. The child can breathe in *So* and breathe out *Hum* aligning the mind of the child with the ever peaceful, unchanging Knower. In this way the child's thoughts and wishes would be sweet and peaceful.

## Om Shānti ॐ शान्ति

The resonance of this mantra is like the cool breeze that rustles the leaves of the *Kalpataru* tree and makes children's thoughts and wishes come true.

## Jai Rām Shrī Rām जय राम श्री राम

As the *Kalpataru* tree fulfills the thoughts and wishes of the mind, this mantra fills the mind with thoughts of victory, perfection and virtue.

## Shiv शिव

This mantra brings the sense of happiness, unity and harmony. It would be a great mantra to repeat when sitting under the *Kalpataru* tree.

## Mantras of your own choosing

You can have great fun with the children helping them select a mantra to be repeated under the *Kalpataru* tree. They may have to think long and hard about their innermost thoughts and wishes. What language do they think in when considering their inner most thoughts?

## The Play of Body, Hatha Yoga

Specific instructions on how to perform the poses can be found in the chapter "The Play of Body, Hatha Yoga."

## Tree Pose वृक्षासन Vrikshāsan

The children can stand tall and steady as if they are magical *Kalpataru* trees.

## Child Pose बालासन Bālāsan

While sitting under the *Kalpataru* tree the boy imagined that friends appeared and played with him. The children can hold the child pose as they imagine that they are playing with their friends.

## Downward-Facing Dog Pose अधोमुखश्वानासन Adho Mukh Shwānāsan

While sitting under the magical *Kalpataru* tree, the boy had many thoughts come true. While performing this pose, the children can pretend to be a puppy playing under the tree.

## Raised Hands Pose ऊर्ध्व हास्तासन Ūrdhva Hāstāsan

As the children raise their hands, you can ask if they can touch the leaves of the *Kalpataru* tree.

## Lion Pose सिंघासन Singhāsan

At the end of the story a lion appears. The children can hold this pose pretending to be the lion from the boy's thoughts.

## Cobra Pose भुजङ्गासन Bhujangāsan

It's a really good thing the boy didn't imagine a cobra while sitting under the magical tree. The children can hold this pose while pretending that they are cobras just passing by.

## Sun Salutation Poses
## सूर्यनमस्कारासन Sūrya Namaskārāsan

The Sun Salutation is a series poses that flow into one another. They are like the series of thoughts that the boy had while sitting under the *Kalpataru* tree.

You can make your own series of poses—a *Kalpataru Namaskār*–where you select poses that flow one into another. It can be a series of the children's thoughts and wishes.

# The Play of Action, Karma Yoga

The instructions for these activities can be found in the chapter "The Play of Action, Karma Yoga."

## Wishing

You can ask the children if they were granted three wishes, what would they be? You can make a list of the children's wishes and ask them where they think wishes come from. You can discuss the changing nature of the mind—why different people have different wishes and even why the same person has different wishes at different times. Thoughts and wishes may come and go, but the one watching them is always there. The one watching them is their own Self, the Knower.

## Timeline

This is a great story for the children to capture the series of thoughts the boy had while sitting under the *Kalpataru* tree. They can illustrate the events on the timeline with or without captions, or they can create a comic strip of their own adventures under the Kalpataru tree. A Timeline and Comic Strip can be found in Timeline "The Play of Action, Karma Yoga."

## Complaint Report

The children can fill out a complaint report about a thought or wish that came true, but not in the way they wanted it to.

## Retell the Story

You can reread the story and stop before the next thought to see if the children can remember what thought comes next.

## Word Power

These activities will empower the children.

**Animated Words:** The children can have fun animating the words from the story.

**Big Words:** Here are some **sesquipedalian words** that relate to this tale.

**befuddle (bih-fuhd-l)**
- unable to think clearly
- to confuse, perplex, bewilder, baffle or muddle

**consequential (kon-si-kwen-shuhl)**
- following as an effect, as a result of, or outcome

**disadvantageous (dis-ad-vuh n-tey-juhs)**
- creating unfavourable circumstances that reduce the chances of success or effectiveness

**extemporaneous (eks-tem-puh-rey-nee-uhs)**
- spoken or done without preparation
- uttered on the spur of the moment

**flabbergast (flab-er-gast)**
- to overwhelm with shock, surprise or amazement

**incomprehensible (in-kom-pri-hen-suh-buhl)**
- not able to understand or comprehend, unintelligible

**phantasmagorical (fan-taz-muh-gawr-i-kuhl)**
  - a fantastical appearance, as something in a dream or created by the imagination

Here are some **sesquipedalian phrases**. Ask the children how they relate to the story.
Surveillance should precede saltation.
(meaning: *Look before you leap.*)

All articles which coruscate with resplendence are not truly auriferous.
(meaning: *All that glitters is not gold.*)

## Memory Games

Included in this section are some amusing memory games that encourage and test children's memories. The games are found in Memory Games, "The Play of Action, Karma Yoga."

## Commercials

The children can make commercials on how to choose wishes, where thoughts come from, how to wish wisely, etc.

## Mirrors

The children can play in pairs or groups. One child would be the leader while the others are the mirrors. The leader can act out three wishes, or three hatha yoga poses, while the others mirror the leader's actions. They can all take turns being the leader.

## Back-to-Back Communication

Two children can sit back-to-back. One is the direction-giver and the other the receiver. The direction-giver would create a picture of her or his wish, then give instructions to her or his partner to see if the receiver can fulfill her or his wish. Then they can switch.

# Timeless Tale 6
# The Bribe

*Some people are very clever. Anywhere you put them they always find a way to be with their habit.*

Once there was a king. In the court of this king there was a man who was in the habit of taking bribes. Everyone in the court knew about this man's habit. No one, not even the king, could figure out how to stop his habit of taking bribes, because the king was governed by a rule that stated, "No one can be fired."

No one could figure out how this man went about getting his bribes. In time everyone just came to know about it. So the king was often wondering what to do about this man and his habit.

One day the king decided to put this man in charge of feeding his horses, the king's special horses. Only that. Just feeding the horses. The food would be delivered to the stables and he would only have to take the food and place it in the horses' troughs.

So what do you think he did?

He overfed the horses and they all came down with tummy aches.

The news of his horses' condition reached the king and the man was called upon to tell the king what the problem was with his horses.

And what do you think he said?

He told the king, "The man who supplies the food for your horses is not a good supplier. You must change suppliers because he is sending inferior food to your horses."

When the supplier of the horses' food heard this, he went to speak to the man who fed the horses. The supplier said, "Here take this money but please do not tell the king the problem is the food. Say that it was something else. You must save me. My supply must continue, I'll pay you money for it."

Thus, the man received his bribe from the supplier of the horses' food.

When the man who feeds the horses was again called before the king, he said that it was not the fault of the supplier. He told the king that he checked the food once again and found that some worms had entered into the food and that was what had created the problem with the horses. Then he said to the king, "Let me check the horses food for one more week. If something goes wrong with the horses, then you should change the supplier, otherwise not."

The king agreed to this.

So for one week the man fed and watered the horses properly. He groomed and brushed the horses, and they all looked healthy and well cared for. After one week had passed, the man looking after the horses went back to the king and told him that the supplier's food was perfectly all right.

...And the man received more bribe money from the supplier of the horses' food.

Now, somehow everyone came to know that the supplier of the horses' food did this, and the man had managed to receive yet another bribe.

The king and his advisors were again wondering what to do about this man.

This time the king decided to give this man the job of counting the waves of the ocean, and he would pay him for that. Now the king thought, "From where will he get the bribe money this time?"

Every day the man would go down to the pier, take out his little boat and anchor it about a mile from the shore. He would sit quietly and do anything he liked. He would eat his sandwiches, look at the sun and the moon and just relax in his little boat. He would never count the waves of the ocean.

But, whenever a ship would pass by, he would pretend to start counting the waves just as the king had told him to do. He would call out to the ship's captain, "Stop there. You cannot pass. I am counting the waves of the ocean for the king. You cannot move your ship until I finish my counting."

Then the captain of the ship would have to deal with this man in order for his ship to continue on its way. The frustrated captain would say, "Now look, you must let my ship pass. Here, take this money, but you must let my ship continue on its route."

...And he would.

*So there are some people who are so intelligent, anywhere you put them they will always find a way to be with their habit.*

# The Lesson
# The Bribe

## Theme

This delightfully amusing tale focuses on the notion of habits. It presents a man whose habit of taking bribes is so ingrained that anywhere he is put, he always finds a way to be with his habit.

Habits can be hard to change and certainly good habits don't need to be changed. In this story the king and his courtiers knew of this man's habit of soliciting and taking bribes. The king, however, was governed by a rule that stated, "No one can be fired." So the king and his courtiers had to figure out different ways to deal with this man and his habit.

From the point of view of the king and his courtiers, taking a bribe was a bad habit. Hard as they tried, they were unsuccessful in encouraging the man to change his habit. They couldn't get him to change because from the man's point of view, the habit of taking bribes was not a bad habit.

Everyone sees from their own point of view which is seen through the filter of their own mind.

## Discussion

This story offers a great opportunity to define and pinpoint what habits are and the role they play in children's lives. Habits are defined by the changing mind and fall into two general categories; they are either good habits or bad habits.

## Dictionary Meanings

**habit:**
- something that you do often and regularly, sometimes without knowing that you are doing it
- an acquired mode of thinking, feeling, behaving or acting that has become involuntary

Regular repetitive thoughts or behaviours can be identified and categorized as being habits. Good habits would be thoughts or behaviours that bring about a child's health, safety and well-being, while bad habits would be detrimental to the child's health, safety and well-being. Normally a person would only consider changing a bad habit. But in order to even consider changing a habit, it first has to be recognized as a bad habit.

When good and bad habits are not clear cut, then making a determination becomes personal and under the purview of the changing mind. This is the focal point of the story. The man who was in the habit of taking bribes did not think that his habit was to his detriment, and so from this man's point of view, this habit was not in need of change. His viewpoint was in contrast to that of the king and his courtiers who were unsuccessful in persuading him otherwise.

> There is nothing either good or bad, but thinking makes it so.
> (William Shakespeare, 1602, *Hamlet*, 2·2)

## Colloquial Expressions

In addition to discussing dictionary definitions, introducing colloquial expressions to the class can enrich the children's experience and help round out their thinking.

### Old habits die hard.

This expression suggests that people find it difficult to change their behaviour or thinking—they are either unable or unwilling.

Over time habits go unnoticed or unchecked because these patterns of thinking or behaving become imprinted in the mind and are then considered normal for that person.

Only bad habits, those that are detrimental to the child's health, safety and well-being, would be considered in need of change. So far as bad habits go, children can learn that they don't have to play victim to bad habits—thoughts or behaviours—rather they can know that they have the strength and freedom to choose what will work for their own well-being.

Through the practice of meditation and placing the attention on the source of who they are, the Knower, they can gain a heightened sense of discrimination which would give them the strength and clarity to gravitate towards choosing their own well-being.

## Suggested discussion questions

- What is a habit?
- Can you think of any habits that you have?
- What is the difference between a good habit and a bad one? What makes a habit good or bad?
- Can you describe some habits?
- Who decides which habits are good or bad?
- Can a habit be good for one person and bad for another?
- What do you understand from the story?
- What do you think about the man's habit of taking bribes?
- What do you think about the law governing the king that states, "No one can be fired"?
- Do you think people should change their habit if it is not good for them?
- Do you think people should change their habit if it is not good for others?
- Where do your habits go when you are asleep?

# Meditation

## Guided Meditation

Have the children sit quietly and comfortably in meditation as you reread the story. Ask them to pay careful attention to the one who is listening to the words.

## Knower Meditation

Ask the children to close their eyes and sit comfortably. They can observe the thoughts that come and go in their minds. You can ask them to pay special attention to thoughts that are more frequent and ask if they would consider these frequent thoughts as mental habits.

If they have a frequent thought that makes them feel bad, ask if they can change it by replacing that thought with one that makes them feel good. You can let them know that they never have to be the victim of a bad thought or a bad mental habit. They have the strength and power to choose to stand for their own well-being.

Ask the children to continue to watch their thoughts come, stay for some time and then disappear from their minds. Remind them to try to place their attention on the one who is watching the thoughts. The one who is watching the thoughts is their own Self, the Knower.

# The Play of Breath, Pranayama

Specific instructions on how to perform the breath exercises are found in the chapter "The Play of Breath, Pranayama."

## Awareness of the Movement of Breath
## प्राण चिन्तन प्राणायाम Prān Chintan Prānāyām

By observing the pattern of their own breathing, children discover what is natural to them before they begin to develop any habits.

## Abdominal Breathing अधम प्राणायाम Adham Prānāyām

Have the children breathe in naturally and pause. Ask them to place their fingers where their breath has paused. Their fingers will most likely point to the chest area. Then have the children breath out slowly. You can point out that this is their natural breathing pattern. For the purpose of introducing this exercise, you can talk about changing the habit of their breathing for just a few breaths.

Ask them to place their fingers on their tummy and see if they can direct the intake of air to where their fingers are. You can talk about how it feels to change a habit, even for just a few breaths.

## Cooling Breath शीतली प्राणायाम Shītalī Prānāyām

When children are caught up in bothersome thoughts that just won't quit, you can suggest that they cool them down with this exercise. The mind and thoughts are linked to the breath, so when the mind is cooled by the breath, the children's thinking becomes pretty cool too.

## Warming Breath सूर्य भेदि प्राणायाम Sūrya Bhedi Prānāyām

When a child's mind is frozen and she or he is unable to make a decision, this warming breath will warm the mind and melt the icy thoughts. Then choice becomes easy.

## Alternate Nostril Breathing
अनुलोम-विलोम प्राणायाम Anulom-Vilom Prānāyām

This breathing technique doesn't let the mind stay with a single habit. It alternates the breath so that it flows with the grain and against the grain. In this way it balances the mind and allows the child to see both sides.

## King of Pranayama
## केवल कुम्भक प्राणायाम Keval Kumbhak Prānāyām

*Keval kumbhak* is the ultimate pause. When children want to change a thought, emotion or habit, they can perform this exercise. You can let the children know that the pause between the breaths gives them the power to choose, rather than just go along with their habit. The point is very subtle. The child may or may not choose the action that belongs to their habit, but it becomes a choice they are making. And making a choice is very empowering.

# The Play of Sound, Mantra

Information and specific instructions on pronunciation of mantras are found in the chapter "The Play of Sound, Mantra."

# Amaram Hum Madhuram Hum अमरम् हं मधुरम् हं

The meaning of this powerful mantra is, "I am immortal, I am blissful." Repeating it helps loosen the grip of the habitual thought and belief that "I am only this." This mantra lets the children know that they are much, much more.

# Shyām श्याम

With the repetition of this very special mantra, children remain untouched by the world of things that cling to them and make them uneasy. Their habit of seeing a glass of water as either half empty or half full becomes transformed. Through repetition of *Shyām* the glass of water overflows drenching them in the light and delight of their own Self, the Knower.

# Om ॐ

This universal sound of peace is a great habit for the children to imbibe.

## Hum हं

The resonance of the sound *hummmm...* unites "I as the individual" with the expanded identity of "I as That." In this way the habit of identifying "I" as being only this, expands to "I as That."

## Mantras of Their own Choosing

It is always wonderful to explore sounds and words that evoke a sense of freedom, peace and love within each child, such as "Pure, Free, Forever," or "I am That, That I am." These mantras can come in all languages and give them the chance to explore and expand the outer reaches of their minds.

# The Play of Body, Hatha Yoga

Specific instructions on how to perform the poses can be found in the chapter "The Play of Body, Hatha Yoga."

## Equestrian Pose अश्व सञ्चलनासन Ashwa Sanchalanāsan

While performing this pose, the children can be like the king's horses when they have been fed and taken care of properly. They can hold their balance as they raise their noble heads.

## Cat Poses मार्जरीआसन/बिडालासन Mārjārīāsan/Bidālāsan

When the children practice these poses, you can suggest that they imagine they are the waves of the ocean, rising and falling allowing all sorts of fish and ships to ride on them. They can count their waves just as the man with the habit was asked to do.

## Raised Hands Pose ऊर्ध्व हास्तासन Ūrdhva Hāstāsan

This energizing pose is known for relieving anxiety. Certainly the ship's captain would have had anxiety when he was stopped by the man with the habit of taking bribes. The captain's reaction would have been to raise his hands in the air. The children can simulate the reaction of the ship's captain as they raise their hands in the air to relieve the captain's anxiety.

## Boat Poses नावासन Nāvāsan

These boat poses build stamina as the children try to navigate the waters without getting stopped by the man who has the habit of taking bribes.

## Gracious Pose भद्रासन Bhadrāsan

The children can sit in the gracious pose and be like the noble king in the story who was ruled by the law that stated, "No one can be fired."

## Child Pose बालासन Bālāsan

The children can rest in this pose and pretend to count the waves of the ocean for the king.

# The Play of Action, Karma Yoga

The instructions for these activities can be found in the chapter "The Play of Action, Karma Yoga."

## Complaint Reports

This activity gives children the opportunity to see from different points of view. You can use the provided Complaint Report and have the children select which character's point of view they would like to represent. A child could take the point of view of one of the horse's who was given bad food just so the man could get his bribe. Another child could represent the captain of the boat or the seller of the horses' food who were forced to give a bribe. A different child could represent the king or one of the king's courtiers who are ruled by the law, "No one can be fired." Another child could represent the man who was in the habit of taking bribes. What would his complaint be?

## Commercials

Children can think of how to make a commercial to advertise an unobvious perception. They can chose their medium—print, television, radio, online—as they devise ways of making commercials for advertising different habits. Who wants to buy a habit!

## Word Power

**Animated Words**: The children can illustrate habits as they animate those words.

**Big Words**: Through learning some big words, the children will come to know that increasing their vocabulary is a power that can be a lot of fun.

Here are some **sesquipedalian words and phrases** to go with the story

**befuddle (bih-fuhd-l)**
- unable to think clearly
- to confuse, perplex, bewilder, baffle or muddle

**bombastic (bom-bas-tik)**
- saying something important sounding with no real meaning
- pompous, grandiose, pretentious

**boondoggle (boon-dog-uhl)**
- an unnecessary, wasteful or fraudulent project or activity often involving graft

**consequential (kon-si-kwen-shuhl)**
- following as an effect, as a result of, or outcome

**idiosyncrasy (id-ee-oh-sin-kruh-see)**
- a characteristic, mode of behaviour or way of thought that is peculiar to an individual

**quintessential (kwin-teh-sen-shul)**
- representing the most perfect or typical example of something

Some suggested **sesquipedalian phrases**:

It is fruitless to indoctrinate a superannuated canine with innovative maneuvers.
(meaning: *You can't teach an old dog new tricks*.)

All articles which coruscate with resplendence are not truly auriferous.
(meaning: *All that glitters is not gold*.)

The person presenting the ultimate cachinnation possesses thereby the optimal cachinnation.
(meaning: *He who laughs last, laughs best*.)

A complete selection is provided in "The Play of Action, Karma Yoga" under the heading "Word Power."

## Doctor's Diagnosis

This activity allows the children to explore different points of view. The children can be paired up, one playing the role of the doctor and the other the role of the patient. The ailments would be of an abstract nature. The patients would be characters from the story, such as the king who might want to know how to deal with his frustration because he is caught between a law that states, "No one can be fired," and having to deal with the man who has a habit of taking bribes. Another patient could be one of the horses who wants to know about how to deal with helplessness because it was fed wrong food just so the man could get his bribe. Other patients could be the supplier of the horses' food or the ship's captain. Each could ask how to cure frustration when they are put in a situation of having to pay a bribe. Do you think the man with the habit of taking bribes would be looking for a cure?

The doctor would interview his or her patient and come up with a remedy or cure for their patient's abstract ailment. Patient Registration and Doctor's Diagnosis forms are provided.

## Grumpy T-Shirt

If you had to pay a bribe you might be grumpy too. Children can express their grumpiness graphically. They can laugh about it as they design their grumpy T-shirt. A paper Grumpy T-Shirt is provided.

## What's on My Mind?

This activity utilizes artistic expression to illustrate "What's on my mind." The children can graphically portray what is going on in their own mind or in the mind of one of the characters from the story.

## Fingerprints

Everyone's fingerprints are unique. The children can have fun developing fingerprint characters. Then they can design a storyboard or comic strip using these fingerprint characters. They can either retell this story or make up their own graphic novel about habits.

# Timeless Tale 7
## The Self Fish

Once a fish came to be in the hands of a boy. And the fish became little.

The boy asked the fish, "What can I do for you?"

The fish answered the boy by saying, "I cannot remain on dry land, I'm a fish. I need to swim in water. I want to swim and swim the whole day long. Could you do something for me?"

"What's that?" asked the boy.

The fish said, "I would like to be put in a glass."

"Well, that's easy enough," the boy responded.

The fish squealed with delight, "Yeah!"

The boy put the fish in a glass filled with water. And the fish was very happy.

Soon the fish grew bigger and filled the whole glass.

Once again the fish spoke to the boy, "I really loved this glass in the beginning. I swam and swam and played in the glass. I could see my reflection in the morning and I would flip my fins and look smart for the whole day. But now the glass is too small for me. I am not comfortable anymore."

The kind boy thought for a moment and then asked the fish, "Would you like me to put you in the tub?"

"Wonderful idea, I would love to be put in the tub," replied the fish in delight.

So the boy carefully placed the fish in the tub. The fish was delighted to play and swim and splash in the tub.

Soon the fish grew bigger and became as big as the tub.

Once again the fish spoke to the boy, "I really loved this tub, but again I grew. I need more space."

The boy pondered over the predicament. Then he said, "Well, there is a river nearby. Would you like to be put in the river?"

The fish became very excited and said, "I would love that. Thank you so much, I would love to be put in the river."

The fish had grown so much that the boy had to get a wheelbarrow to carry the fish from the tub to the river. When they reached the river, the boy carefully placed the fish in the water. The fish gleefully swam and swam and played the whole length of the river, from this end to that.

Soon the fish grew bigger and became as big as the river.

Once again the fish spoke to the boy. "I am not comfortable anymore. In the beginning I loved this river, I swam and swam and played from this end to that. I met so many fish from all different rivers and streams and I had such a good time swimming and swimming and sunbathing. But now, as you can see, I grew again. I am not comfortable."

The boy smiled kindly at the fish and said, "I think it's time to bring you to the ocean."

"I would love that," responded the fish with great excitement. The fish let out a great big sigh of delight, "Ah, the ocean."

The fish had grown so big that the boy had to hire a helicopter to carry the fish from the river to the ocean. In this way the boy placed the fish in the ocean.

Soon the fish grew, and grew, and grew, and grew

and spread...

until...

There was no fish.

There was no boy.

There was no self.

It was all ONE

**SELF**     **FISH**     **NESS**     **!**

# The Lesson
# The Self Fish

## Theme

This humorously delightful tale is a play on words, which deepens with every reading. It symbolizes the growth of awareness—the individual self is represented by the ever-expanding fish who grows and grows and grows and expands to become the whole, the Self, in other words, the Knower.

As the children listen again and again to this delightful tale their understanding transforms along with the fish. As the fish grows in size, the children grow in their awareness of the Knower until they come to know that they are the Knower, they are the Self Fish.

## Discussion

When I would read this story to children, especially for the first time, I was always greeted with squeals of delight and laughter as I came to the final words. The children seemed to intuit the meaning and would often ask for it to be read and reread over and over again. In order to delve deeper into the play on words, knowing and understanding the word meanings is a good place to start.

## Dictionary Meanings

**self:**
- a person's essential being that distinguishes them from others
- the union of elements (such as body, emotions, thoughts, and sensations) that constitute the individuality and identity of a person
- (philosophical) the uniting principle, as a soul, underlying all subjective experience
- (Self as the Knower) the one who is watching, observing, seeing, knowing, we call the Self, or the Knower. It is pure, free, forever and unchanging

**fish:**
- (noun) an animal that lives in water, breathes through gills, has fins and is covered with scales
- (verb) to try to find something; to try to get something without asking directly; to try to lure something

**the suffix -ness:**
- a suffix is attached to adjectives to form abstract nouns that refer to a quality, a condition or state
- the suffix **-ness** exemplifies a quality or state such as, happiness, sadness, nervousness, selfishness, kindness, darkness, etc.

**selfishness:**
- the quality of thinking only of one's own advantage
- (selfishness in reference to the Knower) when the Knower refers to itself as One, or the whole, then selfishness is itself the whole.

This is a very special story in which the individual self, or fish, grows and grows and grows and expands to become the whole, the Knower Self. The children can really have fun with this story because it is so simple, so adorable, so relatable and so very deep.

You can talk with the children about the fish that keeps growing out of its containers—the glass, the tub, the river, the ocean. In the same way, children grow up and grow out of their clothes, their toys, their childish ideas and ways.

You can also talk about abstract or unobvious perceptions, such as the sense of accomplishment. The children can think about how big they feel inside when they have accomplished something monumental. When children feel bigger inside, they look bigger outside. Their outer reflection of bigness is an expression of their inner sense. The children can watch their expansion of awareness grow and grow to become infinite on the inside just as the fish grows to be infinite on the outside.

I think this story is so loved because it expresses everyone's wish to grow in awareness and feel bigger and bigger inside. No one ever wants to feel small.

## Suggested Discussion Questions

- What is a fish?
- What is self?
- How did the boy help the fish?
- Where did the boy place the fish first, second and so on?
- Why did the boy keep placing the fish in larger containers?
- When your body grows bigger and your clothes don't fit anymore, and your toys don't interest you anymore, are you still the same person? How do you know? What has **not** changed?
- What changes and grows?
- Who knows the changes that happen?
- When the fish grew bigger and needed a larger container, did the fish still know how to swim?

- When your body grows bigger, are you still you? What remains the same?
- Who knows that this bigger body used to be a smaller body?
- What is the meaning of selfishness?
- How does selfishness relate to the story?
- Who knows you are you through all the changes that happen to your body and mind?

# Meditation

## Guided Meditation

The children can sit comfortably, close their eyes and listen to the story being reread. They can follow the evolution of the fish as it grows and grows out of container after container. The children can match the expansion of their own awareness with the growth of the fish.

As the body of the little fish expands to infinity, the children can observe their own awareness expand along with it. Ultimately they will come to know that they are infinite and forever in their awareness as the Knower.

## Pranayama Meditation

You can talk to the children about how fish breathe in the water using gills. Have the children imagine that they are fish under water breathing through gills that filter the air from the water. The children can close their eyes in meditation and focus on the awareness of the movement of their breath.

# The Play of Breath, Pranayama

Specific instructions on how to perform the breath exercises are found in the chapter "The Play of Breath, Pranayama."

## King of Pranayama
## केवल कुम्भक प्राणायाम Keval Kumbhak Prānāyām

When the fish grew and grew and grew to become the whole, the Self Fish, it became the only one—*Keval* means the only one. If the children watch the space between their breaths, that is where they will find the Self Fish.

## The Sound of Om प्रणव प्राणायाम Pranav Prānāyām

Noises are heard differently underwater. As fish travel through water they hear sound waves and feel their vibrations. It is said that goldfish listen to music. Have the children imagine they are underwater listening to the swishing of the water and waves. Have them listen carefully and ask if they can hear the sound of the Self Fish.

## Chanting Breath उद्गीथ प्राणायाम Udgīth Prānāyām

Start by selecting a mantra, for example *Om* or Home. The children can start off quietly chanting the mantra on their exhalation with their natural voice. On the next round they can chant the mantra on a higher note. With every round of chanting the mantra, the children can raise the note higher and higher, just like the fish who got bigger and bigger. When the exercise is complete, the children will most definitely end on the highest note.

## Victory Breath or Ocean Breath
## उज्जायी प्राणायाम Ujjayī Prānāyām

While performing this exercise you can ask the children to pay attention to the sound of the ocean as they slowly breathe out through their left nostril while blocking their right. They can also keep their attention on breathing in and breathing out just as a fish breathes underwater.

## Humming Bee भ्रमरी प्राणायाम Bhramarī Prāṇāyām

When practicing this exercise the children can pretend that the sound they exhale is that of a mythical underwater Humming Fish. Underwater Humming Fish communicate with other fish through their humming sounds.

## Awareness of the Movement of Breath
## प्राण चिन्तन प्राणायाम Prān Chintan Prāṇāyām

Children breathe with lungs and fish breathe underwater with gills. The children can watch as they breathe in filling their lungs with air and then breathe out emptying them. Have them sit and watch the process of their own breathing and become aware of its rhythm. They should be the Knower of their own breath.

## The Play of Sound, Mantra

Information and specific instructions on pronunciation of mantras are found in the chapter "The Play of Sound, Mantra."

## Amaram Hum Madhuram Hum अमरम् हं मधुरम् हं

This mantra is a revelation, the sound from the source. As the little fish grows and grows and expands to become the whole, the Self Fish, it merges with the sound of the source, *Amaram Hum Madhuram Hum.* Repetition of this mantra is like the fish repeating its own name.

## Om ॐ

*Om* is the mantra of peace. It is said that *Om* encompasses the entire Devanagari Alphabet (the alphabet in which Sanskrit is written). The mantra *Om* or *Aum* is the Devanagri version of A-Z. The entire alphabet is contained in the sound *Om.* The children can try to imagine the little fish growing to include every word in existence—at least every word that uses the letters of the alphabet. Can the children think of any word that doesn't use a letter from the alphabet?

## Shyām श्याम

This exquisite mantra represents the blue-black space, the depths of the ocean. Through repetition of this mantra, the children's awareness will locate the Self Fish.

## Hum हं

*Hum* means "I as That." The little fish grows and expands from "I the little fish" to "I as That, the Knower, the Self Fish."

## So Hum सो हं

This exercise reflects the sound of the breath. The children can inhale *So* as the little fish and exhale *Hum* as the Self Fish.

## Mantras of your own choosing

The children can have fun selecting a mantra that grows and grows and grows and relates to their own sense of humour. For example, "Space, I need Space," "Space, Space, I need Space," "Space, Space, Space, I need Space." The children can keep adding a little extra "space" to their mantra. They can also have fun adding "space" in many different languages.

# The Play of Body, Hatha Yoga

Specific instructions on how to perform the poses can be found in the chapter "The Play of Body, Hatha Yoga."

## Forward-Fold Pose उत्तानासन Uttānāsan

This forward fold pose can be likened to the graceful way a fish dives in the water.

## Gracious Pose भद्रासन Bhadrāsan

When children hold this gentle gracious pose, they can be likened to the way fish glide effortlessly through water.

## Boat Poses नावासन **Nāvāsan**

The children can pretend to be a boat gliding on the surface of the water occasionally stopping to talk to a fish.

## Bow Pose धनुरासन **Dhanurāsan**

In this bow pose the children can pretend to be a fish doing the back stroke. Have you ever seen a fish do the back stroke? There is always a first time.

## Cat Poses मार्जरीआसन/बिडालासन **Mārjārīāsan/Bidālāsan**

The children can pretend to be a fish playing in the waves, swimming up and down as they complete the two parts of this pose. The children can also pretend to be the rise and fall of the ocean waves.

## Corpse Pose or Immortal Pose शवासन **Shavāsan**

In this restful pose the children can contemplate the quiet depths of the ocean where there is no movement, just quiet contemplation.

# The Play of Action, Karma Yoga

The instructions for these activities can be found in the chapter "The Play of Action, Karma Yoga."

## Retell the Story

This story can be retold in tandem with the growth of the child's awareness. You might like to combine this with Timeline and use the timeline as a visual aide for this activity.

**Note:** Children grow up. As they grow in awareness the children grow out of concepts and ideas that once confined and limited them. They learn, evolve and become aware that they are the Knower of this awareness. They come to know that all the phases of life—baby, toddler, teenager, adult and golden ager—may appear differently, but the one who lives the phases, is one and the same. In this way they come to know that there is no baby, no toddler, no teenager, no adult and no golden ager. The one who knows all the changes does not change. The one who knows this is One. ONE, SELF-FISH-NESS, the Knower.

## Timeline

This activity focuses on linear thinking. The children can make a visual representation, on a timeline or comic strip, of how the fish started in the hands of the boy, was placed in the glass, the tub, the river, the ocean and then... You can incorporate this activity with "Retell the Story."

The children can create their own comic strip or graphic novel depicting the growth of awareness.

## My World

This unique activity measures the height of each child as the size of their world. Each child starts out as one little fish. As the children join their worlds or measured strings to other children's worlds, the world they create grows and grows and grows as all are included in one world or one Self-Fish-Ness.

## Commercials

The growth of the fish is symbolic of the growth in awareness. Growing to infinity in awareness is not measured in physical size, it is measured by how peaceful and at ease a child is in her or his own skin. It is interesting to observe that as the fish grew it became uncomfortable in its former encasement. Once placed in a larger, more appropriate container, the fish immediately became happy and at ease. Children can make commercials to showcase the growth in awareness, the feeling of achievement, the sense of love and compassion and so forth.

## Word Power

The children can learn how words can grow and grow. Here are some **sesquipedalian words** that relate to the story.

**anthropomorphism (an-thruh-puh-mawr-fiz-uhm)**
- the attribution of human characteristics or behaviours to an animal or object

**Brobdingnagian (Brob-ding-nag-ee-uhn)**
- gigantic, huge, of immense proportions
- *Brobdingnag* is the imaginary land of giants in *Gulliver's Travels*, by Jonathan Swift. It is always written with a "B."

**cryptozoology (krip-toh-zoh-ol-uh-jee)**
- The search for and study of animals whose existence or survival is disputed or unsubstantiated, such as the Loch Ness monster and the yeti.

**flabbergast (flab-er-gast)**
- to overwhelm with shock, surprise or amazement

**humongous (hyoo-muhng-guhs)**
- huge, enormous, extraordinarily large

**phantasmagorical (fan-taz-muh-gawr-i-kuhl)**
- a fantastical appearance, as something in a dream or created by the imagination

**zenith (zee-nith)**
- highest point, topmost, peak, apex, summit

Some enjoyable **sesquipedalian phrases**:

If an enclosure for a pedal extremity adapts itself suitably to said appendage, it would be advisable to employ it accordingly.
(meaning: *If the shoe fits, wear it.* )

Members of an avian species with identical plumage will congregate.
(meaning: *Birds of a feather flock together.*)

The stylus is more potent than the dirk.
(meaning: *The pen is mightier than the sword.*)

You can also let the children have fun **animating words**. They can illustrate how the words can grow and grow and grow.

## Blowing bubbles

Blowing bubbles is one of the many things that fish love to do. The children can have fun blowing bubbles, watching how their breath interacts with water.

## Broken Telephone

In the game of broken telephone the initial word or message that is whispered, becomes transformed with every whispering. It's like a story that gets bigger and bigger with every telling.

## Mala (with Mantra)

The children can enjoy counting the beads using a mantra as they watch their conscious awareness grow and grow.

# Timeless Tale 8
## Truth Story

*You may have heard people say, "Don't tell lies." It means try to avoid trouble. When people say, "Speak the truth," it means recount the story exactly as it happened. This world is such that after some time, you may get confused and then you will not be able to distinguish what is a lie from what is the truth.*

One day a hunter spotted a deer grazing in a meadow. The deer knew it had been spotted by the hunter. In order to save its life, the deer took off and ran quickly into the forest. The hunter in quick pursuit.

In the forest the deer ran past a man who was meditating under the shade of a tree. The man opened his eyes as the deer ran past and watched as it disappeared into the thicket. He then closed his eyes and continued to meditate.

The hunter soon approached the man who was sitting quietly meditating. He asked, "Have you seen the deer? Tell me, which way has it gone?"

The man who had been meditating slowly opened his eyes. He was now faced with a dilemma, what should he say?

The man who had been meditating knew that this man was a hunter and would kill the deer if he found it. He thought for a moment. Then told the hunter, "No, I have not seen any deer. While I was meditating I think I heard the sound of a deer running through the bushes towards the river side." He pointed the hunter in the opposite direction from where the deer had gone.

The hunter then set off through the bushes in the direction of the river. Thus, the man who had been meditating saved the life of the deer by telling a lie to the hunter.

When the hunter reached the river and found no trace of the deer, he turned back, retraced his steps and once again reached the man who was meditating under the tree. Again the hunter spoke to the man, "You seem to have told me a lie. The deer has not gone through these bushes towards the river side. Tell me the truth, which way has the deer gone?"

The man remained quiet. Then he closed his eyes and continued to meditate. The hunter became frustrated and left. This time he went in the direction of the thicket, the direction that the deer had really gone.

There the hunter came across another man who was meditating in the forest under the shade of a tree. The hunter asked this man, "Have you seen the deer? Tell me, which way has it gone?"

This man thought to himself, "I have seen the deer, but if I tell the hunter I have not, I will be punished for telling a lie." In order to avoid being punished, he decided to tell the hunter the truth. "Yes, I have seen the deer. It has gone this way." He pointed in the direction the deer had gone to seek refuge from its pursuer.

With the help of this man, the hunter soon came across the deer. The hunter shot it, and the deer died.

Thus, the man who told the truth became the cause of the deer's death, and the man who told the lie saved the life of the deer— even if it was only for a short while.

*So what is good and what is bad? What is a lie and what is the truth? This world is such that after some time you may get confused. Then you will not be able to distinguish what is a lie from what is the truth. In this life you have to trust your own wisdom.*

# The Lesson

## Truth Story

## Theme

Truth Story presents the children with a dilemma two men are faced with. The two men must each decide whether to tell the truth or to tell a lie. Each man makes his own decision. This story offers a unique opportunity for children to explore the deeper meaning of the concepts—What is a lie? What is the truth? and What is wisdom? In a safe environment, the children can discuss and explore the idea of making hard choices when difficult situations are confronted.

It is important to remind the children that the nature of the mind is changing. It fluctuates between what it considers right and what it considers wrong. Wisdom is found in the unchanging peace of the Knower. The children can reach inside to seek clarity and guidance in the wisdom of their own Self, the Knower.

## Discussion

Presenting the dictionary meanings of words provides a clear and level playing field for understanding. This story presents a dilemma for children to think and talk about. I have always found this story to be quite stimulating so far as group discussions are concerned. You can really have some very lively and insightful discussions with the children.

## Dictionary Meanings

**truth:**
- in accordance with fact or reality
- a fact or belief that is accepted as truth
- sincerity in action, character and utterance

**lie:**
- to say or write something with deliberate intent to deceive
- an intentionally false statement

**wisdom:**
- the ability to use your knowledge and experience to make good decisions and judgements

You can lead class discussions towards watching the mind. Ask the children to observe the mind's debate between the two notions: "What is a lie?" and "What is the truth?" These concepts are grounded in "What is good?" and "What is bad?" "What is right?" and "What is wrong?" And most importantly, "Am I good?" and "Am I bad?" They can observe the changing nature of the mind in light of the pairs of opposites. The children can be reminded that the one watching the changes of the mind is forever unchanged. The unchanging observer goes by the name of Knower.

## Suggested Discussion Questions

- What is the meaning of the word "truth" and What is the meaning of the word "lie"?
- Have you ever told a lie because you were afraid to tell the truth?
- What have you understood from the story?
- What were the problems in the story?
- How do you feel about the man who told the truth?
- How do you feel about the man who told the lie?
- How do you feel about the hunter?

- Is there a higher truth? What would that be?
- What does wisdom mean?
- What would you have done? Why?
- Has anything like this ever happened to you?
- When you are asleep where have the truth and the lie gone?
- When you are asleep where have the deer and the hunter gone?
- What do you think the story is really about?
- What do you think it means to have wisdom?

# Meditation

## Mantra Meditation

Mantra is the instrument that releases the mind from the thoughts and ideas that bind it to uneasiness. The power of mantra focuses the mind as it engages it in thoughts of peace, unity and freedom. The mantra *Rām* attracts the sense of success and happiness. It is very simple to repeat, *RāmaRāmaRāmaRām*.

If they like, you can help the children select their own mantra for this meditation.

## Pranayama Meditation

Meditation using "Awareness of the Movement of Breath" will focus the children's mind on their breath. They can breath in to "what is a lie," pause to wisdom, breath out to "what is the truth," pause to wisdom and so forth. In this way they will observe that the movement of breath, both in and out as well as the pause, all come from the same breather.

## Mala Meditation

Mala meditation is a tactile approach that is very helpful to focus the children's attention on either counting the beads, counting mantras or counting breaths. It gives the mind focus and time to be absorbed in the peace of meditation. For more detailed instructions on the use of the mala please see "Mala" in the chapter "The Play of Action, Karma Yoga."

## The Play of Breath, Pranayama

Specific instructions on how to perform the breath exercises are found in the chapter "The Play of Breath, Pranayama."

### Abdominal Breathing अधम प्राणायाम Adham Prānāyām

This exercise places the attention on breathing deeply. Ask the children to place their fingers on their tummy and then try to guide their breath towards their fingers. You can let them know that wisdom is hiding in the depths of their breath and they can guide their mind to where wisdom resides by breathing deeply.

### Chanting Breath उद्गीथ प्राणायाम Udgīth Prānāyām

The children can breathe in slowly and deeply through their nose and pause for a second or two. As they slowly exhale through their mouth, they can chant the mantra *Om*, Home or any mantra that they think will bring peace to those meditating and dwelling in the forest.

### Alternate Nostril Breathing
### अनुलोम-विलोम प्राणायाम Anulom-Vilom Prānāyām

This exercise alternates between going with the grain and against the grain. The pairs of opposites are represented by the changing nature of the mind with the questions, "What is the truth?" and "What is a lie?" When the children pause their breath and change nostrils, that pause is *kumbhak*, that pause is wisdom, that pause is the Knower.

## Balanced Breathing
## सम-वृत्ति प्राणायाम Sam-Vritti Prānāyām

The children can balance their breathing with this exercise. They can imagine a square. Ask them to inhale on the first side and think of the word "lie," then pause on the bottom imagining "wisdom," they can exhale on the other side to "truth" and pause on the top side to "wisdom." The sides of the square are changing—inhaling and exhaling—representing the mind with the words "lie" and "truth." The top and bottom or the foundation and roof of the square represent the unchanging wisdom of the Knower.



## Shining Forehead
## कपालभाति प्राणायाम Kapālbhāti Prānāyām

This exercise brings about the wisdom of the Knower. As the children energetically exhale the mind's sense of duality—truth and lies—their faces become shining with the light of the wisdom of the Knower.

## King of Pranayama
## केवल कुम्भक प्राणायाम Keval Kumbhak Prānāyām

While performing this exercise the children rest in the pause between the inhalation and the exhalation. That pause is the peace and wisdom of the Knower.

# The Play of Sound, Mantra

Information and specific instructions on pronunciation of mantras are found in the chapter "The Play of Sound, Mantra."

## Amaram Hum Madhuram Hum अमरम् हं मधुरम् हं

When *Amaram Hum Madhuram Hum* is repeated, the unchanging truth and wisdom of the Knower is revealed. That is why this mantra is always a great choice.

## Om ॐ

The mantra *Om* is the fundamental sound of the universe, including all the changes the mind experiences. The one repeating *Om* watches as truth and lies become only points of view of the changing mind. The one who watches the changes is forever unchanging and peaceful, and goes by the name Knower.

## Om Shānti ॐ शान्ति

This beautiful mantra is the invocation of peace on earth. It can be practiced by repeating the word *Shānti* (peace) three times. *Om Shānti Shānti Shānti*. The children can practice wisdom by repeating this mantra.

## So Hum सो हं

This mantra echoes the sound of the breath. The children can inhale to *So* as "What is a lie?" pause to wisdom, exhale to *Hum* as "What is the truth?" and pause to wisdom. As they do so they can place their attention on the one who is breathing and repeating the mantra *So Hum*. The one breathing and repeating the mantra is their own Self, the Knower.

## Hare Krishna Hare Rām हरे कृष्ण हरे राम

This mantra celebrates liberation from bondage. It heightens the power of discrimination as the children come to know for themselves what truth is, what a lie is and what wisdom is.

## Jai Rām Shrī Rām जय राम श्री राम

Perfection and virtue are accomplished through this mantra as it celebrates the victory of good over evil. This mantra celebrates wisdom.

## Mantras of your own choosing

The children can take their time and think about an appropriate mantra for this story. An example would be "Trust in wisdom, Trust in wisdom" in many languages.

# The Play of Body, Hatha Yoga

Specific instructions on how to perform the poses can be found in the chapter "The Play of Body, Hatha Yoga."

## Tree Pose वृक्षासन Vrikshāsan

This pose represents balance and focus. You can ask the children to perform this pose pretending to be trees in the forest. They will have to make a choice which leg to stand on, they can only choose one at a time.

## Corpse Pose or Immortal Pose शवासन Shavāsan

Lying in this pose the children can pretend to be the deer who has met its demise. They can contemplate, from the deer's point of view, the notions: "What it means to tell the truth" and "What it means to tell a lie."

## Cat Poses मार्जरीआसन/बिडालासन Mārjārīāsan/Bidālāsan

In this two part pose, the children can pretend to be the deer running away from the hunter.

## Downward-Facing Dog Pose
## अधोमुखश्वानासन Adho Mukh Shwānāsan

The children can pretend to be a downward-facing deer as it plans its escape from the hunter.

## Equestrian Pose अश्व सञ्चलनासन Ashwa Sanchalanāsan

The children can pick a point in the room to stare at in order to help maintain their balance and focus as they lunge into the knowledge and understanding of "What is a lie," "What is the truth" and "What is wisdom." In this pose they can be the deer.

## Bow Pose धनुरासन Dhanurāsan

In this bow pose the children can pretend to be the bow that the hunter uses to let his arrow fly.

## Lion Pose सिंघासन Singhāsan

The lion represents power, strength and wisdom. This pose is great for placing the attention on making important decisions.

## Sun Salutation Poses
## सूर्यनमस्कारासन Sūrya Namaskārāsan

These lovely flowing movements can be performed as sequences from the story. You can also create your own flow of movements, your own "Truth Story Salutation Poses" by selecting hatha yoga poses that describe the story.

# The Play of Action, Karma Yoga

The instructions for these activities can be found in the chapter "The Play of Action, Karma Yoga."

## Complaint Report

This activity offers children the chance to isolate events and bring into focus different points of view. The children can fill out the provided complaint report from the point of view of a story character. For example the hunter could fill out a report complaining about the lack of cooperation he received from the first meditating man. Each of the men meditating could fill out a complaint report about their meditation being interrupted and the difficult position they were placed in. The deer could fill out a report complaining that the hunter was pursuing it, just because it was a deer.

## Timeline

The children can use the provided timeline or comic strip to recreate the events of the story. This can be combined with Fingerprints. The children can use their fingerprints to create the story characters.

## Fingerprints

Everyone's fingerprints are unique. Everyone's understanding is also unique. You can have the children examine their own fingerprints as well as the fingerprints of their friends. They can combine this activity with "Timeline" where the children retell the story using their fingerprints to create the characters.

## Mirrors

The children can reenact the story in hatha yoga poses or their own style of movement. One child can create the pose while their friends mirror their movements.

## Broken Telephone

This is a group activity in which one child starts out with a word or phrase that is whispered to the child next to him or her. This child whispers what he or she has heard to the next child and so on, until all the children have had the chance to hear and pass along what they have heard. The last child to hear the word or phrase then says it aloud. Then in opposite order the children reveal what they had heard. It is always humorous to find out how the truth of a word or phrase changes as it is whispered around the room.

You can ask the children what made what they heard the truth, and what made what someone else heard (if different) a lie. What each child heard was simply what each one heard.

## Word Power

Words have power. This activity showcases the power of communication skills.

### Animated Words:

The children can animate words from the story such as tree, meditate, deer, truth and lie, etc.

### Big Words:

**Sesquipedalian words** and phrases are always fun. Here are some for this story.

**consequential (kon-si-kwen-shuhl)**
- following as an effect, as a result of, or outcome

**disadvantageous (dis-ad-vuh n-tey-juhs)**
- creating unfavourable circumstances that reduce the chances of success or effectiveness

**discombobulate (dis-kuhm-bob-yuh-leyt)**
- to confuse someone or make someone feel uncomfortable

**euphemism (yoo-fuh-miz-uhm)**
- The substitution of a mild or inoffensive expression for one that may offend, embarrass or suggest something unpleasant.

**widdershins (with-er-shinz)**
- counter-clockwise or anti-clockwise, describing the opposite direction from the way a clock moves
- in the opposite or contrary direction from usual

Some **sesquipedalian phrases**.

Missiles of ligneous or petrous consistency have the potential of fracturing my osseous structure, but appellations will remain sempiternally innocuous.
(meaning: *Sticks and stones can break my bones, but names will never hurt me.*)

If an enclosure for a pedal extremity adapts itself suitably to said appendage, it would be advisable to employ it accordingly.
(meaning: *If the shoe fits, wear it.*)

It is futile to become lachrymose over precipitately departed lacteal fluids.
(meaning: *Don't cry over spilled milk.*)


## Mala

The children can meditate with a mala just as the two men meditated under the tree. Each man meditating came to a different conclusion. You can ask the children to meditate with a mala on "What is wisdom."

They can also choose to count the beads or meditate on each bead using the mantra *Amaram Hum Madhuram Hum*.

# Timeless Tale 9

## What Is an Elephant?

*We all see from our own point of view and remain convinced of our own rightness. This story shows that being right, doesn't have to mean that someone else is wrong.*

There were four blind men who enjoyed exploring together. One day they came across an elephant. None of these men had ever encountered an elephant before. They elected one among them to approach the elephant in order to let the others know what an elephant is.

When the first blind man approached the elephant, he encountered its head. The elephant extended its trunk and the blind man gently stroked it with his hand. To his companions he declared, "An elephant is like a snake, long and thick and bending."

The second blind man became curious, he too wanted to know what an elephant is. As the second man approached he was greeted by the elephant's tusks. This blind man's experience was different from his friend's. The second blind man spoke out in disagreement saying, "You are not right, an elephant is not at all like a snake. An elephant is like a smooth bamboo branch."

This disagreement compelled the third blind man to approach the elephant in order to bring clarity to their disagreement. The third man encountered the elephant's leg. He declared, "No, no, you are both wrong. An elephant is not like a snake, nor is it like a bamboo branch. An elephant is like a pillar, round and thick and tall."

In order to settle this dispute, the fourth blind man decided to approach the elephant. This man encountered its backside and experienced the swish of the elephant's tail. This man declared, "You are all wrong. An elephant is not like a snake, a bamboo branch, or a pillar. An elephant is like many ropes swishing though the air."

They all began to argue. No one could agree. Each blind man was convinced that he was right and that everyone else was wrong.

Now as it happened a man with sight had been meditating nearby. When he heard the commotion he opened his eyes. There he saw the elephant standing quietly still, and the four blind men arguing. He decided to approach them.

In order to shed light on their disagreement, the man of vision declared that each of them was very correct. This created more confusion and a great commotion. They couldn't understand how they all could be right. How could an elephant be like a snake, a bamboo branch, a pillar and many swishing ropes, all at the same time?

The man of vision explained, "The first blind man approached the head of the elephant and encountered its trunk, which is very much like a snake, long and thick and bending."

The man of vision continued, "The second blind man encountered the tusk of the elephant, which is as he described like a smooth bamboo branch. The third blind man reached the leg of the elephant, which he correctly described to be very much like a pillar. And the fourth encountered the tail of the elephant, which is very much like the swishing of many ropes."

The man of vision paused for a moment and then continued. "So what is an elephant? Based on your own individual experiences, each of you was very correct in your knowledge and understanding. But each of you experienced only that much. You could not experience the elephant as a whole."

*This story shows that we all see from our own point of view. People may be convinced of their own rightness, but it doesn't mean that other people must be wrong.*

*The Knower is like an infinitely large elephant where every mind sees only a part of it. It takes the expanded vision of the Knower to see the whole elephant.*

# The Lesson
## What Is an Elephant?

## Theme

Everyone sees from their own perspective and everyone remains convinced that their own thoughts and conclusions are the only correct ones. The mind is a changing mechanism that receives its input from the senses and believes what it receives and perceives to be the truth. This story shows that everyone's mind functions in the same way—every mind believes in its own rightness. The story also demonstrates that believing in your own rightness doesn't mean that others must be wrong in their perception.

At the end of the story it states that the Knower is like an infinitely large elephant where every mind sees only a part of it. This story demonstrates how people are blinded to the infinite knowledge of the Knower by the limited perception of their own mind.

**Note**: On their own, eyes do not have the power to see. If the eyes are sitting in a jar or in a dead person, those eyes do not have the power to see. The power to see comes from the Knower. The rest is how you deal with it.

## Discussion

This story is a metaphor about what it means to be blind to the knowledge of the truth—the inability to see beyond the experience of the mind and senses. This inability made the four men blind to the elephant as a whole and to any other point of view.

## Dictionary Meanings

**blind:**
- lacking the sense of eyesight
- unable or unwilling to discern or judge
- not controlled by reason
- to refuse to notice something that is obvious to others

**elephant:**
- Elephants are large five-toed pachyderms (thick skin) with several distinctive features. The most notable is their long trunk that they use for many purposes; breathing, lifting water and grasping objects. Their incisors grow into tusks, which can serve as weapons and as tools for moving objects and digging. Elephants have large ear flaps that help to control their body temperature. Their pillar-like legs carry their great weight. Their swishing tails drive away pesky insects. Elephants are often thought to bring good luck.

## Colloquial Expressions

Here are some common expressions to explore. You can even have the children come up with their own expressions.

**An elephant never forgets.**
Elephants are known to have great memories. This expression refers to a person with an excellent memory.

**An elephant in the room.**
This means there is a big issue everyone is aware of that is being ignored, because everyone finds it too uncomfortable to talk about.

**When a pickpocket sees a saint, all he sees are his pockets.**
People see what is already in their mind's perception or whatever they are preoccupied with.

**You never have to change what you see, only the way you see it.**
This story demonstrates that it is not what the blind men experience that needs to change. Gaining vision is what is needed.

## Suggested Discussion Questions

- Do you know what an elephant is?
- What does it mean to be blind?
- What makes your ideas or experiences right? How do you know?
- What makes someone else's experiences wrong?
- How does it feel when someone tells you that you are wrong?
- What have you understood from this story?
- What did each blind man understand about what an elephant is?
- What made each blind man convinced of his own rightness?
- Who do you think was right in the story?
- Is it possible to see from someone else's viewpoint?
- Where do thoughts, ideas and concepts come from?
- Do your thoughts, ideas and concepts change?
- What happens to your thoughts and ideas when you are asleep? Where do they go?
- If you had a dream about an elephant, how would such a big animal fit inside your head?
- What did the man of vision have that the blind men didn't have?
- Who watches the changing thoughts and dreams as they appear in your mind?

# Meditation

## Guided Meditation

You can reread the story as the children close their eyes in meditation. They can quietly contemplate what it means to be blind and what it means to have sight.

## Knower Meditation

The children can close their eyes and watch as their thoughts come and go and change. Their changing thoughts are springing from their changing minds. Ask the children to observe the thoughts as they change. Ask them who knows the changes? You can let them know that the one who knows and watches the changes is "you." The "me, I or you" inside each of us is unchanging and goes by the name Knower. The children can meditate on the Knower.

# The Play of Breath, Pranayama

Specific instructions on how to perform the breath exercises are found in the chapter "The Play of Breath, Pranayama."

## Abdominal Breathing अधम प्राणायाम Adham Prānāyām

When the children perform this full yogic breath their tummies will puff out like an elephant. They can pretend to be like the elephant standing tall and grand with its trunk, tusks, legs and tail.

## Bellows Breath भस्त्रिका प्राणायाम Bhastrikā Prānāyām

The elephant's ears help regulate the temperature of their large body. While performing this exercise, the children can pretend that the bellows are the elephant's ears moving forward on the inhale, pause, backward on the exhale, pause, thus making the elephant more comfortable.

## Chanting Breath उद्गीथ प्राणायाम Udgīth Prānāyām

This breath exercise can be a tribute to the elephant as the children exhale the sound that elephants make.

## Shining Forehead कपालभाति प्राणायाम Kapālbhāti Prānāyām

The children can take a slow deep breath in, pause, and as they breathe out energetically they can imagine the elephant's trunk lifting. They can lift their arm pretending it is a trunk.

## Humming Bee भ्रमरी प्राणायाम Bhramarī Prānāyām

When the children practice this exercise they can pretend that the sound emanating from them is the sound of elephants humming. Have you ever heard of a humming elephant?

# The Play of Sound, Mantra

Information and specific instructions on pronunciation of mantras are found in the chapter "The Play of Sound, Mantra."

## Amaram Hum Madhuram Hum अमरम् हं मधुरम् हं

This very beautiful mantra is a revelation that can guide the children to their own true Self, the Knower. By repeating this mantra the children will see the elephant as a whole.

## Hum हं

The children can repeat the mantra *Hum*, which means "I as That." *Hum* is described as the sound of the space that is before the utterance "I." It represents the original space that stands by itself, just like the elephant.

## Om Shānti ॐ शान्ति

An elephant never forgets. The children who repeat *Om Shānti Shānti Shānti* will never forget the peace that's inside them.

## Om Rām Shiv Shyām ॐ राम शिव श्याम

This lovely four part mantra can represent each of the four blind men; *Om* representing the first man, *Rām* the second, *Shiv* the third and *Shyām* the fourth.

## Mantras of your own choosing

The children can experiment with words and sounds that bring about the vision of the Knower, for example "Pure, Free, Forever." They can have fun finding out the translation of their chosen mantra in different languages.

# The Play of Body, Hatha Yoga

Specific instructions on how to perform the poses can be found in the chapter "The Play of Body, Hatha Yoga."

## Mountain Pose ताडासन Tādāsan

The children can stand tall and sturdy, like the elephant who was approached by the four blind men

## Cobra Pose भुजङ्गासन Bhujangāsan

In this cobra pose the children can pretend to be the trunk of the elephant.

## Tree Pose वृक्षासन Vrikshāsan

While performing this pose the children can be the tusk of the elephant which is like a smooth bamboo branch.

## Gracious Pose भद्रासन Bhadrāsan

The children can relax in this pose and be like the man of sight quietly sitting in meditation and seeing all the men and the elephant as they are.

## Raised Hands Pose ऊर्ध्व हास्तासन Ūrdhva Hāstāsan

As the children raise their hands upwards, they can imagine being a tall pillar, like a leg of the elephant.

## Corpse Pose or Immortal Pose शवासन Shavāsan

In this pose the children can quietly contemplate the story and what it means to them.

# The Play of Action, Karma Yoga

The instructions for these activities can be found in the chapter "The Play of Action, Karma Yoga."

## Blindfold Games

In these blindfold games the children have the opportunity to explore the five senses and see what it means when one sense, the sense of sight, is unavailable to them.

## Back-to-Back Communication

The children can be reminded of the blind men's communication skills, and how they tried to convince each other of their own rightness. In this activity each child should take a turn being the direction-giver and the receiver. This provides each child with the chance to know how it feels to give directions and to take them.

## Timeline

The children can graphically illustrate this story or create one of their own, showing how misunderstanding or a difference of opinion can be transformed by gaining a broader perspective. If they like, they can add captions to their illustrations.

## Word Power

### Big Words:

The power of words should never be underestimated. It represents the power to express, articulate and communicate thoughts and ideas. It is always delightful to watch children expand their vocabulary with **Big Words**. Here are some **sesquipedalian words** to go with this story.

**befuddle (bih-fuhd-l)**
- unable to think clearly
- to confuse, perplex, bewilder, baffle or muddle

**Brobdingnagian (Brob-ding-nag-ee-uhn)**
- gigantic, huge, of immense proportions
- *Brobdingnag* is the imaginary land of giants in *Gulliver's Travels*, by Jonathan Swift. It is always written with a "B."

**extemporaneous (eks-tem-puh-rey-nee-uhs)**
- spoken or done without preparation
- uttered on the spur of the moment

**hodgepodge (hoj-poj)**
- a confused mixture of different things

**humongous (hyoo-muhng-guhs)**
- huge, enormous, extraordinarily large

**incomprehensible (in-kom-pri-hen-suh-buhl)**
- not able to understand or comprehend, unintelligible

**pandemonium (pan-duh-moh-nee-uhm)**
- wild and noisy disorder or confusion, an uproar

**zenith (zee-nith)**
- highest point, topmost, peak, apex, summit

Some **sesquipedalian phrases**

Members of an avian species with identical plumage will congregate.
(meaning: *Birds of a feather flock together.*)

Surveillance should precede saltation.
(meaning: *Look before you leap.*)

The stylus is more potent than the dirk.
(meaning: *The pen is mightier than the sword.*)

## Memory Games

An elephant never forgets. These suggested activities can be adapted for all ages. The children can enjoy matching their memory skills with their friends to see who remembers most like an elephant.

# Bibliography


A.A. Milne, 1927, *Now We Are Six*

Benjamin S. Bloom, 1956, *Taxonomy of Educational Objectives: The Classification of Educational Goals*

Dictionary meanings from:
dictionary.com,
dictionary.cambridge,
en.oxforddictionaries.com,
merriam-webster.com,
wikipedia.org.

Dr. Seuss, 1971, *The Lorax*

Dr. Seuss, 1990, *Oh, The Places You'll Go!*

F. Scott Fitzgerald, 1925, *The Great Gatsby*

J.K. Rowling, 1997, *Harry Potter and the Philosopher's Stone*

Lewis Carroll, 1865, *Alice in Wonderland*

Lord Byron, 1819, *Don Juan*

Oscar Wilde, 1893, *Lady Windermere's Fan*

Robert Louis Stevenson, 1883, *The Silverado Squatters*

Swami Shyam, 1974, *The Sovereign Secret of Meditation*

Swami Shyam, 1975, *Mastermind*

Swami Shyam, 1983 *Why Meditation*

Swami Shyam, 1985, *Bhagavad Gita: The Most Precise and Comprehensive Rendering*

Swami Shyam, 1994 *Vision of Oneness*

Swami Shyam, 2012, *Highest Wishfulfiller Meditation Explained*

Swami Shyam, 2015, *You Are Never Ignorant of Your Self*

William Shakespeare, 1595 *Romeo and Juliet*

William Shakespeare, 1599, *Julius Ceaser*

William Shakespeare, 1602, *Hamlet*

William Shakespeare, 1611 *The Tempest*

William Shakespeare, 1623, *As You Like It,*

# Detailed Contents


Foreword — 8

How to Use This Book — 10

Prologue — 15

**Part 1: Curriculum & Instruction** — 21

**Chapter 1—The Play of Philosophy, Darshan, Direct Experience** — 23

The Mind — 24

The Knower — 26

Meditation — 31

**Chapter 2—The Play of Breath, Pranayama** — 38

Awareness of the Breath — 39

Pranayama Exercises — 41

- Awareness of the Movement of Breath प्राण चिन्तन प्राणायाम Prān Chintan Prāṇāyām — 42

- Abdominal Breathing अधम प्राणायाम Adham Prāṇāyām — 44

- Balanced Breathing सम-वृत्ति प्राणायाम Sam-Vritti Prāṇāyām — 45

- Alternate Nostril Breathing अनुलोम-विलोम प्राणायाम Anulom-Vilom Prāṇāyām — 46

- Warming Breath सूर्य भेदि प्राणायाम Sūrya Bhedi Prāṇāyām — 48

- Victory Breath or Ocean Breath
  उज्जायी प्राणायाम Ujjayī Prānāyām **49**

- Cooling Breath शीतली प्राणायाम Shītalī Prānāyām **50**

- Shining Forehead कपालभाति प्राणायाम Kapālbhāti Prānāyām **51**

- Bellows Breath भस्त्रिका प्राणायाम Bhastrikā Prānāyām **52**

- Humming Bee भ्रमरी प्राणायाम Bhramarī Prānāyām **53**

- Chanting Breath उद्गीथ प्राणायाम Udgīth Prānāyām **54**

- The Sound of Om प्रणव प्राणायाम Pranav Prānāyām **55**

- King of Pranayama
  केवल कुम्भक प्राणायाम Keval Kumbhak Prānāyām **56**

# Chapter 3—The Play of Sound, Mantra **58**

## Mantras **61**

- Amaram Hum Madhuram Hum अमरम् हं मधुरम् हं **62**

- Om or Aum ॐ or ओम **62**

- Om Shānti ॐ शान्ति **63**

- Hum हं **63**

- So Hum सो हं **63**

- Rām राम **64**

- Jai Rām Shrī Rām जय राम श्री राम **64**

- Shiv शिव **65**

- Shyām श्याम **65**

- Hare Krishna Hare Rām हरे कृष्ण हरे राम **65**

- Om Rām Shiv Shyām ॐ राम शिव श्याम **66**

- Mantras of your own choosing **66**

## Chapter 4—The Play of Body, Hatha Yoga — 67

### Hatha Yoga Poses — 70

- Mountain Pose तााडासन Tādāsan — 70
- Tree Pose वृक्षासन Vrikshāsan — 71
- Forward-Fold Pose उत्तानासन Uttānāsan — 72
- Equestrian Pose अश्व सञ्चलनासन Ashwa Sanchalanāsan — 73
- Raised Hands Pose ऊर्ध्व हास्तासन Ūrdhva Hāstāsan — 74
- Downward-Facing Dog Pose अधोमुखश्वानासन Adho Mukh Shwānāsan — 75
- Cat Poses मार्जरीआसन/बिडालासन Mārjārīāsan/Bidālāsan — 76
- Bow Pose धनुरासन Dhanurāsan — 77
- Boat Poses नावासन Nāvāsan — 78
- Lion Pose सिंघासन Singhāsan — 79
- Bridge Pose सेतुबन्धसर्वाङ्गासन Setu Bandh Sarvāngāsan — 80
- Gracious Pose भद्रासन Bhadrāsan — 81
- Sphinx Pose सलम्ब भुजङ्गासन Salamb Bhujangāsan — 82
- Cobra Pose भुजङ्गासन Bhujangāsan — 83
- Child Pose बालासन Bālāsan — 84
- Corpse Pose or Immortal Pose शवासन Shavāsan — 85
- Warrior Poses वीरभद्रासन Vīrabhadrāsan — 86
- Sun Salutation Poses सुर्यनमस्कारासन Sūrya Namaskārāsan — 89

## Chapter 5—The Play of Action, Karma Yoga 92

### Activities and Games 94

- Back-to-Back Communication 94
- Balance Scales 96
- Blindfold Games 97
  - *What Is It?* 97
  - *Open Locks Blindfolded* 97
  - *Drawing and Writing Blindfolded* 97
- Blowing Bubbles 98
- Broken Telephone 99
- Building Bridges 100
- Coat of Arms 102
- Commercials 105
- Compass and Mapmaking Skills 107
  - *How to make a Compass* 107
  - *Compass Activities* 108
  - *A Compass Game* 108
  - *Mapmaking and Map Planning* 109
- Complaint Report 110
- Doctor's Diagnosis 112
- Family Tree 115
- Fingerprints 117
- Grumpy T-Shirt 118
- Mala 121

- **Memory Games** — **123**
  - *Memory Cards* — **123**
  - *Three Cups* — **123**
  - *Word Chain* — **124**
  - *Memory Match* — **124**
- **Mirror Breath** — **125**
- **Mirrors** — **126**
- **My World** — **128**
- **Name Games** — **130**
  - *What's In A Name* — **130**
  - *Name Game* — **130**
  - *Describe Yourself* — **131**
  - *My Name* — **131**
- **Prediction Activities** — **132**
  - *Fortune Cookies or Fortune Cakes* — **132**
  - *Astrology* — **133**
  - *Paper Fortune Tellers* — **136**
- **Retell the Story** — **138**
- **Timeline** — **139**
  - *Comic Strip* — **140**
- **What's on My Mind?** — **141**
- **Wishing** — **142**
- **Word Power** — **143**
  - *Animated Words* — **144**
  - *Big Words (Sesquipedalian Words)* — **145**
  - *Sesquipedalian Phrasess* — **148**

**Part 2: The Play of Words, Implementation** **151**

The Play of Knowledge, Gyan Yoga 152

Timeless Tales and Their Lessons 157

Timeless Tale 1—Cunning Mr Monkey 159
   The Lesson 162

Timeless Tale 2—Destiny 172
   The Lesson 176

Timeless Tale 3—Donkey Riding 188
   The Lesson 191

Timeless Tale 4—Fox and Camel 202
   The Lesson 208

Timeless Tale 5—Kalpataru 221
   The Lesson 224

Timeless Tale 6—The Bribe 235
   The Lesson 238

Timeless Tale 7—The Self Fish 249
   The Lesson 252

Timeless Tale 8—Truth Story 263
   The Lesson 265

Timeless Tale 9—What Is an Elephant? 276
   The Lesson 279

Bibliography 288

# Afterword

I want to thank you for your interest in teaching meditation to children and hope you have enjoyed reading this book as much as I have enjoyed writing it.

I spent many delightful years and hours researching, compiling and putting this book together—converging my knowledge of curriculum development with meditation, the yogic disciplines, insightful stories and child development. When I was writing this book, I felt as though I was pouring all my knowledge and years of experience into its pages so that I could share it with you.

I have always believed that the inner light in each and every child could be cultivated, nurtured, fostered and revealed through guiding and developing the mind, body and spirit of the child so that each one could blossom and grow into their very best and unique self. And I believe this can happen through meditation on the Knower.

I would like to appreciate those who have offered their time and encouragement to me and to the creation of this project.

I want to thank my teacher Swami Shyam, who encouraged me to write, to collect insightful stories and to create a curriculum for teaching meditation to children.

I want to appreciate Dr Helen Amoriggi and Dr Heather Trump from the Department of Education of McGill University. Their encouragement and belief in me has stayed with me all these many years.

To all my expert friends who helped in so many ways:

I want to thank Susan Cowan who offered her time and editorial expertise. She poured over every single word of this manuscript with loving dedication.

Many thanks to Dr Glen Kezwer for his Foreword and his editorial skills. I want to express my gratitude to my expert consultants on the yoga disciplines: Ruth Bacal for pranayama, Filomena DiBratto for mantra and Anabel Littledale for hatha yoga. Thanks to Barbara Sager and Dr Stephen Thompson for their Sanskrit assistance.

I also want to appreciate Eric Myhr who taught me how to format this book, Stephen Aitken who gave me valuable tips on digital illustrating, Ann Lardner for her artistic advice and Ellen Reitman for her photographic expertise.

Thanks to Jarrett Astrof and Pip Jarden who listened to every story and every lesson. We giggled and laughed our way through all the pages and words and had so much fun doing it!

My extra special thanks to Jarrett who made this project come alive.

Thank you to all my friends who offered their love and support to this project. Especially to Stephen Astrof, Sherrie Wade, Ellen Rosenberg, Gadi Karmi, Juhi Srivastava and Grady May for their continued encouragement.

I absolutely enjoyed every moment I spent in the creation of this curriculum. I hope you, your children and all those with whom you share this book, will delight in it as well.

Enjoy!

Shelley Astrof

Shelley Astrof

# About the Author

Shelley Astrof is from Montreal, Canada. She has her Master of Education degree from McGill University, Canada; Doctor of Meditation from Vishwa Unnyayan Samsad, India; Certificate of Advanced Studies in Yog Science, Vedant Philosophy, and the Theory and Practice of Meditation from the International Meditation Institute, India. In addition she was awarded Peace Pioneer from the International Meditation Institute.

She taught elementary school in both the public and private sectors of Montreal and ran a small school in India. During her time at McGill University she worked on numerous research projects as well as teaching off-campus B.Ed. courses in the James Bay Region of Northern Quebec. In addition she worked as a tutor on film sets for child actors.

In the many years she spent studying and teaching meditation and Vedant philosophy, one of her main hobbies was collecting and writing insightful stories for children everywhere.

Her love for children, education, meditation and storytelling has been combined in this unique approach to teaching meditation to children.

www.ingramcontent.com/pod-product-compliance
Lightning Source LLC
Chambersburg PA
CBHW080512030726
47592CB00012B/3325